Emotional Intelligence - Life Mastery

Practical Self-Development Guide for Success in Business and Your Personal Life-Improve Your Social Skills, NLP, EQ, Relationship Building, CBT & Self Discipline.

By Ewan Miller

Table of Contents

Emotional Intelligence – Life Mastery
Table of Contents
Introduction
Chapter 1: Understanding Emotional Intelligence

   Emotional intelligence versus intelligence quotient
   Emotional intelligence versus social intelligence
   Emotional intelligence in psychology
   A brief history of emotional intelligence
   Other research and studies on emotional intelligence
   Emotional intelligence framework
   High and low emotional intelligence
   Why developing emotional intelligence is crucial
   Self and relationship management
   Emotional intelligence in the workplace
   Emotional intelligence and relationships

Chapter 2: The Application of Emotional Intelligence

   Handling Impulses
   Handling difficulties and setbacks
   Handling stress and anxiety
   In the workplace
   Coping with trauma
   Coping with reactions

Chapter 3: Recognizing Emotions

   Envy
   Worry or nervousness
   Anger or aggravation
   Dislike
   Disappointment or unhappiness

Chapter 4: Improving Emotional Intelligence

    Emotional intelligence in the relationship
    Body language
    Active listening
    Mindfulness and relaxation techniques

Chapter 5: Emotional Intelligence and Leadership

    Good leadership
    Adaptation
    Leadership and performance
    The six styles of leadership
    How to improve
    The five components of emotional intelligence in leadership
    Social skills

Conclusion

Introduction

If you were looking for a book on emotional intelligence that is highly practical and offers a guide for success in business and personal life than this is the right book. The book delves onto social skills, emotional quotient, relationship building, self-discipline and cognitive behavior therapy using simple to understand language. Using easy and relatable examples, the author introduces what constitutes emotional intelligence, why it differs from the intelligent quotient and offer ways of improving social skills at work and home using emotional intelligence. For this reason, this book is both a manual and a discussion of applicable emotional intelligence for beginners and seasoned individuals.

In uniformly spaced subtopics, the author guides the reader on how to apply emotional intelligence by handling impulses, managing setbacks, and handling stress and anxiety. The book walks the reader through applying emotional intelligence at the workplace, handling trauma, and coping with reactions. The reader is taken through ways of recognizing emotions especially the common and negative emotions at the workplace. Some of the common and negative emotions explored are anger, nervousness, unhappiness, and dislike. Emotionally intelligence is also applied in relationships and in leadership and the reader is exposed to how emotional intelligence affects leadership and relationships as well as how to enhance emotional intelligence.

Chapter 1: Understanding Emotional Intelligence

Emotional intelligence versus intelligence quotient

The individual ability to evaluate, identify, manage and express emotions is known as emotional intelligence. Persons with high emotional intelligence are likely to make efficient leaders and team players since they possess the ability to empathize, understand, and link with people around them. On the other hand, intelligent quotient evaluates academic abilities and identifies persons with mental challenges or persons with exceptional abilities. At the workplace, emotional intelligence is a widely accepted indicator of success to help acknowledge good team players, leaders, and independent workers.

In detail, intelligence quotient captures abilities such as fluid reasoning, knowledge of the world, spatial and visual processing, quantitative reasoning, and working memory and short-term memory. On the other hand, emotional intelligence captures the way of relating to others, identifying emotions, assessing how others feel, managing individual emotions, and perceiving how others feel as well as employing emotions to enable social communication. Initially, intelligence quotient was seen as the fundamental determinant of success as persons deemed to have high intelligence quotient were seen as destined for accomplishments. All this led to a debate about whether intelligence is a product of the environment or gene factors.

With time critics started to acknowledge that high intelligence is not a guarantee for accomplishment in life. Additionally, intelligence quotient alone could not capture the full spectra of human abilities and knowledge. When it comes to academic achievement intelligent quotients is still accepted as a critical element of success. Persons with high intelligent quotients are likely to excel in school and earn more money as well as having a healthier life. Contemporary experts acknowledge that intelligent quotient is not the only determinate of success in life. Against this backdrop, the intelligent quotient is seen as integral of an intricate array of influences that include emotional intelligence.

Equally important is that the concept of emotional intelligence has had a significant impact in a number of areas especially the business domain. Most organizations now demand emotional intelligence training and employ emotional quotient tests as integral to the hiring process. Persons with effective leaders tend to exhibit high emotional intelligent insinuating that a high emotional quotient is a critical component of business leadership and management.

An illustration can be when you take an insurance company that realizes that emotional intelligence can play a critical role in the success of sales. It then emerges that sales agents that rank lower on emotional intelligence abilities such as empathy, self-confidence, and initiative tend to sell an average premium of $45, 000 compared to those agents that rank high on emotional intelligence scores that sell an average of $105, 000.

Additionally, emotional abilities can be used to impact the choices that consumers make when faced with buying decisions. Most people prefer to deal with an individual that they trust and like compared to someone they do not and this implies paying more for an inferior product.

Indeed emotional intelligence can be learned. Some of the ways that emotional intelligence can be imparted are through character education, encouraging people to think about how others are feeling, modeling positive behaviors, and discovering ways to be more empathetic toward others. Like any other form of coaching, the candidate for training should be willing to gain knowledge and practice it. A person seeking to enhance his or her emotional intelligence levels should first do a self-evaluation of weaknesses that relate to emotional intelligence and then do more evaluation using the guideline of an expert. When coaching someone on emotional intelligence, it should be implemented gradually and adjusted to the individual needs of the candidate.

In overall, both intelligent quotient and emotional quotient play critical roles in impacting the overall success of an individual including wellness, health, and happiness. Learning to improve the skills in weak areas to more than average is important than just focusing on the gifted areas. The reason for this argument is that as an individual, your whole is more important than the specific strengths. Think of it this way, you are a highly intelligent worker but unable to handle disappointments which compromise your overall productivity. Alternatively, think yourself as a highly emotionally stable person and have the unique ability to engage others but have difficulties learning new technologies and systems at the workplace which ends up affecting your overall productivity. Ideally, having a balance of the intelligent quotient and emotional quotient is highly beneficial. Fortunately, there are proven methods to help work on your weak areas to make you whole.

Exercise

a. As part of the hiring team looking for a replacement of an Information Technology Officer at your company, you only managed to shortlist two candidates where one of the candidates is a sharp person with respect to academic accomplishments but appears temperamental. The other is average in academics but appears emotionally stable and warm to engage. How would you handle the hiring process to end up with the most suitable candidate for your organization?

b. Get any episode of Bing Bang Theory TV series and make a first impression of Sheldon Cooper character. Assume that only observation is enough to judge an individual, would you hire Sheldon Cooper? Why and Why not?

Emotional intelligence versus social intelligence

Emotional intelligence relates to the present and emotions manifesting. For instance, a mother knows how the baby is feeling. The mother knows if the baby is sad or hungry. Alternatively, think of a shy and scared teenager at a party. You managed to perceive this because you have emotional quotient applied appropriately. On the other hand, social intelligence concerns more about the future as you are relying on present knowledge to enhance the future by looking for the best pathway for you. For instance, a worker in an organization that looks for a different way to disagree with the boss on the new measures being implemented.

In this manner, social intelligence concerns comprehending the personalities and corresponding behaviors of people to understand how to best get along. The intent of social intelligence is to precipitate positive outcomes from interactions between people. On the other hand, emotional intelligence concerns helping an individual become aware of his emotional status and manage it to make him or her more relatable. Taking all this into account, emotional intelligence is a prerequisite of social intelligence where social intelligence is the derivative of the former. Simply put, without a person having requisite emotional intelligence levels he or she is likely to perform poorly in social interactions. Think of Sheldon Cooper in the TV series Big Bang Theory.

The further explanation includes acknowledging that social intelligence is when emotional intelligence is applied in a group setting making everyone comfortable, accommodative and civil. For this reason, social intelligence has evolved to enable us to survive. Think of survival and accomplishment at your career requires more than just good grades. For instance, you might be highly qualified but respond poorly to questions seeking to ascertain your emotional stability. In other terms reacting rudely at your interviewers constitutes a signal that you have low social intelligence level. Lack of manifesting requisite social intelligence can increase the risk of losing jobs, opportunities or friendship.

An illustration of social intelligence may be the case of Richard who is a stereotypical office employee. Richard is socially intelligent enough to comprehend that his boss is offended at casual bad news. For this reason, Richard understands that it is socially intelligent to phrase negative news in a way that begins with positive aspects of the news to avoid triggering an emotional reaction from his boss. On the other hand, Richard understands that if he shares the news with Juliet that she will casually share it and does not think about the consequences of her actions when spreading the news. Against this backdrop, Richard employs socially intelligent and avoids telling Juliet to save when the news is wholly positive.

Additionally, Richard employs emotional intelligence in conference meetings. Now assume that everything is going well at his Tuesday meeting but suddenly he notices facial expressions on Juliet that indicates that she is feeling irked and agitated. Richard then adjusts the delivery and notices that Juliet is now calm and settled with the suggested project but remains mum. It is through emotional intelligent that Richard manages to seek the opinion of Juliet on the project. Juliet provides her opinion and this helps to constructively move the project forward as they both reach a consensus. The above two illustrations demonstrate the functional difference between emotional intelligence and social intelligence.

For further emphasis, emotional intelligence requires certain competencies that include the following; self-awareness that addresses emotional awareness, self-confidence and self-assessment. Emotional intelligence also requires one to possess self-regulation that includes adaptability, innovativeness, self-control, conscientiousness, and trustworthiness. The other component of emotional intelligence includes self-motivation that covers commitment, drive, initiative, and optimism. Emotional intelligence requires one to be exhibit social awareness that addresses service orientation, empathy, leveraging diversity, developing others, and political awareness. Finally, emotional intelligence requires exhibiting social skills that include leadership, communication, conflict management, change management, and cooperation. All these are the comprehensive areas of emotional intelligence training that one needs.

Finally, social intelligence concerns the competence that helps an individual relationship with others. Social intelligence can be split into relationship-management and social-awareness. All these sub-concepts can be studied differently from the main concept, social intelligence that has been dubbed emotional and social intelligence. Rightly, social intelligence is a derivative of emotional intelligence. In this manner, social intelligence extends emotional intelligence. The purpose of this emphasis is to enable trainers and candidates to understand what should precede the other. Emotional intelligence coaching should precede social intelligence training. In simplest terms, you have to understand and manage yourself before you can positively engage other people.

Exercise

a. How can you enhance your social intelligence at school or workplace?

b. Think of a politician that has difficulties relating with others and suggest five ways the politician can improve his or her social skills.

Emotional intelligence in psychology

Various researchers affirm the assertion that several personality disorders are mediated or moderated by the emotional intelligence of an individual. In the context of psychology, emotional intelligence concerns sets of skills to facilitate, acknowledge, comprehend, and manage emotions that allow the use of emotional knowledge to attain a higher adjustment as well as psychological wellbeing. By having a high emotional intelligence you are likely to have a positive frame of mind, are likely to redress your mood after adverse emotions as well as score lower on stress, anxiety, and depression.

Notably, the connection between emotional intelligence and psychology is supported by the realization that patients with several clinical disorders show deficits in emotional intelligence score. The assumption that we form here is that a low score in emotional intelligence suggests varied potency for clinical disorders. For instance, various studies assert that most attention deficit individuals show a deficit in any of these emotional competencies. The other assumption that we make here is that emotional intelligence competencies contribute to the development and maintenance of the attention deficit.

Patients with social anxiety show a strong correlation between the seriousness of the symptoms and the difficulty to sufficiently perceive emotions and employ them to facilitate their thinking.

Furthermore, individuals with pathological demand avoidance condition exhibit significantly lower scores in emotional understanding and management skills compared to the healthy control group participants. All these indicate that deficit deficits in emotional understanding and integration are integral in the phenomenology of panic disorder. Individuals with general anxiety disorder focus more on their emotions and have critical difficulties in addressing their negative moods. Persons with general anxiety disorder degree of symptoms are related to their difficulties to clearly differentiate between various emotional states. The implication of this assertion is that perceived incapacity to manage your individual emotions could be a susceptible factor in the development of generalized anxiety disorder.

Against this backdrop, challenges with managing emotional states are a critical indicator of potentiality for personality disorders. In some nonclinical subjects, pathological personality traits are linked to critical deficits in emotional intelligence such as schizotypal, psychopathic, and borderline traits. It can then be argued that the presence of personality disorders in patients with attention deficit can be linked to higher deficits in emotional intelligence.

Correspondingly, emotional intelligence is critical to developing a balanced life. Emotional intelligence is not restricted to only communicating with people. Emotional intelligence should be treated as an avenue to realize a balanced-life. Every aspect of life requires emotional intelligence. For instance, emotional intelligence impacts physical health which is the ability to care for our bodies. By managing the stress that has a significant effect on our wellness we are acknowledging the critical role of emotional intelligence. By being aware of our emotional state as well as our reactions to stress we can hope to handle stress and maintain good health.

Expectedly, emotional intelligence affects our mental well-being by impacting our outlook and attitude on life. Emotional intelligence can aid in alleviating anxiety and avoid depression and mood swings. With this in mind, a high level of emotional intelligence directly correlates to a positive attitude as well as a happier outlook on life. We are better at communicating our feelings in a more helpful manner through comprehending and handling our emotions. In this manner emotional intelligence impacts relationships. Through emotional intelligence, we manage to comprehend and relate to others that we have interactions with. It is through understanding feelings, needs, and reactions of those we care about that inform stronger and more satisfying relationships.

Similarly, emotional intelligence impacts conflict resolution. It is through discerning the emotions of other people that we learn to empathize with their views of the issue making it easier to resolve conflicts or avoid the conflicts before they fester. The ability to comprehend the needs and desires of other people increases our efficiency at negotiation. Emotional intelligence also impacts success as higher emotional intelligence assists us to be assertive effective internal motivators that can help lower procrastination, enhance self-confidence, and enhance our ability to concentrate on a goal. Emotional intelligence can enhance our potentiality for success by enabling us to build better networks of support, conquer challenges, and preserve with a more robust outlook. In overall our ability to delay gratification and take into consideration the long-run directly impacts our ability to succeed.

Unfortunately, emotional intelligence in psychology also has a negative side. The danger of emotional intelligence is that it is morally neutral implying that it depends on how one uses it. Emotional intelligence can be charged and used by an individual to attain ulterior motives at the expense of others. Emotional intelligence can be used as an Asperger in which the individual may not understand what others are feeling. Emotional intelligence in a psychopath makes the individual not to care what you are feeling even though the individual is aware. Lastly, a Machiavellian manipulates how you feel to accomplish selfish ends. For Asperger Syndrome think of Sheldon Cooper of the Big Bang Theory TV series. Finally, persons with a high level of deception are likely to be the dominant members in a group setting and make the others merely pawns in helping the leader accomplish selfish ends.

Exercise

a. In your own terms explain how emotional intelligence links with psychology?

b. Do you agree that emotional intelligence scores correlate with various clinical personality disorders? Why and why not?

c. Try to link the aspect of deception as increasing the likelihood of the deceptive individual being a leader/dominant member of a group. Explain using public figures or celebrities or TV characters.

A brief history of emotional intelligence

Emotional intelligence as a separate construct did not exist until 1953 where Dorothy Van Ghent observed in her book exploring the Pride and Prejudice English novel that most of Jane Austen characters in the book exhibited a high emotional quotient. A German psychoanalyst, Barbara Leuner in 1966 argued that the drug LSD could help women with low emotional intelligence and at that time Leuner held the view that low emotional intelligence arose due to early separation from mothers that led to more emotional problems compared to the control group. However, the first individual to state the term emotional intelligence in an English language source was Wayne Payne through the 1986 dissertation. Wayne applied the term widely in his dissertation suggesting that emotional awareness was a critical component to develop in children.

Accordingly, it is the psychologists Mayer and Salovey that aligned with contemporary usage of the theory of emotional intelligence by offering the first formulation of the concept and an illustration of how emotional intelligence can be evaluated in two journal articles in 1990. During this period of the early 1990s, the concept of intelligence quotient was widely acknowledged as the gold standard of excellence in life. Equally important is that during this period the debate largely dominated around whether intelligent quotient was wired in our genes or acquired from the environment through individual experience. It was until 1995 that Daniel Goleman as a science reporter discovered Mayer and Salovey's studies and started to feel motivated by the thinking that there could be a novel way of viewing the components of life achievement.

Identically to Mayer and Salovey, Goleman employed the term emotional intelligence to capture a wide spectrum of scientific findings that drew together separate subdomains of research. The work of Goleman also covered other related scientific developments like the field of neuroscience which at its infancy at the time explored how emotions are managed in the brain. When Goleman published his work dubbed Emotional Intelligence and why it can count more than intelligence quotient in 1995, it gained global attention. During this period, most health professionals had not come across the idea of emotional intelligence despite Mayer and Salovey's studies being out for five years. So popular was the concept of emotional intelligence that Goleman's works became the best seller and impacted the world in several ways.

Additionally, Goleman noted that he felt elevated by hearing that educators had embraced emotional intelligence in the form of what is known as social and emotional learning. At the time of the seminal works of Goleman premiering; only a few schools ran programs teaching emotional intelligence skills to students. UNESCO in 2002 began a global initiative to promote social and emotional learning by developing ten fundamental principles for operationalizing social-emotional learning to at least 140 countries' ministries of education. They have been a number of attempts to evaluate the impact of direct instruction on a person's ability to exhibit emotional intelligence. In overall, some studies have exhibited significant success in measuring emotional intelligence while the other studies critique if emotional intelligence merits as a valid construct.

Notably, Mayer, Goleman, and Salovey proposed the notion of emotional intelligence partly due to the recognition of the unfair hegemony that the evaluation of intelligent quotient enjoyed at the period. There is a likelihood that they knew of persons with high intelligence but were not regarded as successful. Think of how in the contemporary workplace words such as nerd and geek still elicit much admiration. In essence, these slang terms describe an individual that is socially inadequate. So far it is convincing to assert that emotional intelligence competencies will impact the productivity of an individual, especially in teamwork setups.

Lastly, commanding a huge intelligence quotient attributes does not guarantee a person a satisfying human relationship and inner peace. Instead, such qualities are widely exhibited in the case of persons that have high emotional intelligence as well. For instance, a high intelligence quotient may enable a person to get shortlisted for a dream job but without emotional intelligence, the candidate may fail to impress at the interview stage. The example given illustrates how emotional intelligence may enhance the likelihood of success of an individual. The conclusion should be that emotional intelligence and intelligence quotient complement each other.

Exercise

a. In your opinion, who made a significant impact in drawing the world attention to the concept of emotional intelligence?

b. Do you hold the view that emotional intelligence proponents appear to subtly degrade the criticality of intelligence quotient?

Other research and studies on emotional intelligence

Recent studies on emotional intelligence share insight into how general intelligence and emotional intelligence affect student's academic and social abilities. From recent studies, it emerged that both general mental ability and emotional intelligence have an effect on the academic and social performance of students in college. However, general mental ability played a significant role in predicting academic performance compared to emotional intelligence. Another interesting discovery is that only emotional intelligence, as opposed to general mental ability, was related to the quality of social interactions with peers. We can argue that emotional interaction is required to enable you to work with others and indeed work with the public that prioritizes how you handled them compared to how smart you are. From these assertions, possessing more than average of emotional intelligence and intelligence quotient increases the likelihood of an individual excelling in school and at the workplace.

Additionally, recent research on emotional intelligence explored the individuals with schizophrenia if they exhibit impaired emotional intelligence in comparison to a control group and seeks to pinpoint the exact emotional intelligence areas of weakness in the case that the assertion holds. From current studies, persons with schizophrenia performed significantly worse compared to controls. The common areas of weaknesses for persons with schizophrenia included understanding, identifying, and managing emotions. Having low emotional intelligence scores was significantly correlated with increased difficulties in community functioning of an individual. The suggestion with this research is that emotional intelligence competencies can be used to help improve the life quality of individuals with various psychological conditions. Emotional intelligence can be used to further detector further improve existing mental illnesses, especially where personality disorders exist.

Furthermore, contemporary studies on emotional intelligence explore if emotional intelligence can be taught and if so can the information derived by an individual get retained over time. Some of the recent studies affirm that training groups on emotional intelligence will improve their emotional intelligence competencies. From the current studies finding, emotional intelligence competencies were still retained after six months. The implication of these studies and their findings is that emotional intelligence can be acquired and enhanced. Compared to intelligence quotient, emotional intelligence is highly coachable and also can be retained. Another implication of this study is that employers now have more freedom when hiring as they can still recruit a highly skilled individual and enroll the candidate for emotional intelligence training enabling the organization command a well-balanced workforce in terms of intelligence quotient and emotional intelligence competencies.

Lastly, new research on emotional intelligence focuses on the relationship between emotional intelligence and job performance. The connection between emotional intelligence and productivity was explored concentrating on the intersection between self-and other-focused emotional intelligence dimensions. Several studies affirm that emotion appraisal plays a significant role in subjective and objective job performance. As suggested above, emotional intelligence can help the question of why there is a gap in hiring a highly skilled candidate that has difficulties delivering perhaps due to challenges with working with others, communicating how he feels, and being tolerant. Most organizations deal with the public directly where how the organization communicates and handles a client counts more in some cases compared to the efficacy of the solution given.

Finally, current studies explore the possibility of emotional intelligence overlapping with personality and cognitive traits. Emotional intelligence tends to co-vary with cognitive abilities as well with personality traits. One of the other critical areas in human resource management is correct personality typing. Emotional intelligence can help increase correct personality typing compared to using only personality typing tests. Unlike personality tests, emotional intelligence measures actively profile the personality of a candidate. Emotional intelligence tests can infuse both ability and trait models of testing which can help correlate with the personality of an individual. There is a need in the future to investigate if emotional intelligence score correlates with cognitive and personality traits. For emphasis, the ability model of emotional intelligence enables evaluation of cognitive traits of an individual while the trait model aligns more with the personality of an individual.

Exercise

a. Assume that you are part of the board seeking to hire a candidate to replace the former network engineer at your Information Technology consultancy company. For this position, skills are highly critical as the successful candidate must actually perform the technical competencies specified. At the same time, the successful candidate has to work with others and train them on the organizational systems. It is apparent that you will require an individual that has significant mental abilities as well as emotional intelligence. After careful elimination, you have Richard, a highly skilled network engineer but appears to be emotionally unstable when asked questions that seem basic or offensive. On the other hand, you have Mike who has average skills and appears an average learner but has a great personality. As the final person, briefly describe how you would navigate this situation by prioritizing the company needs. Remember the needs of the company include getting a competent individual that must also work with others with ease.

Emotional intelligence framework

The emotional intelligence framework constitutes of three models that are the trait model, the ability model, and the mixed model. All these model focus on the application of knowledge and power to impact your emotional intelligence even though they differ significantly.

Starting with the ability model, it is an emotional intelligence framework that concerns perceiving emotions by understanding nonverbal signs such as the facial expressions of other people. The emotional intelligence framework also includes reasoning with emotions as emotional intelligence enhances thinking including a cognitive activity. Understanding emotions imply that one is interpreting the emotions of others around you and getting to acknowledge that people express emotions of anger when essentially they might not be angry at you but the situation. With respect to the ability framework, a person learns to manage emotions and react appropriately and consistently. For this reason, the ability framework uses self-awareness, self-regulation, motivation, empathy and social skills.

Secondly, there is a mixed framework that integrates different kinds of emotional intelligence qualities. Through this framework, we combine knowledge and understanding that concerns emotion triggers. Another aspect of the mixed approach is that it also covers skills such as empathy. Mixed approach framework concerns competencies such as the ability to detect facial expressions. There are also other components of the mixed model that include traits such as being optimistic and attitudes such as service orientation. Where possible, this model can also include other qualities such as being inspirational. It is challenging to assess all the aspects of emotional intelligence with one instrument and this call for the need to mix a variety of tools within one mega tool and then create an emotional quotient score.

Equally important when evaluating the mixed framework is how to process the proportion of each emotional intelligence basic tool that should be included. For example, do you use more items from the ability framework or from the trait framework? Another concern is how these combinations will impact the final outcome as each input data vary even though it is leading to the same objective. The proponents of this framework argue that it enables one to leverage on the strengths of each model and reduce the limitations of each individual model.

Additionally, there is the trait framework which largely constitutes self-reportage tools. Critics of this emotional intelligence framework think that self-perception is unreliable enough lest the tool is being used for personal reflection. It might be difficult to ascertain well how you perform at discerning your emotions and handle them as a type of thinking that gets clouded when having emotional meltdowns if your emotional intelligence is great. The major role of trait tools is that they will help you recognize how you view others and interact with them from an emotionally intelligent perspective. The focus on self-reportage is qualified because individuals are likely to relapse to inborn traits and self-reportage effectively brings this out.

Individuals that work in the domain of human behavior experience challenges about the believability of self-report concerning mental states. Usually, the issue of subjective experiences tends to dominate much of self-reportage that invites the question of bias. Individual bias impacts how he or she views others. Emotionally intelligence is a collection of competencies and skills that improve the performance of an individual at the workplace. In this manner, emotional intelligence should be handled as an interlinking of behavior motivated by social and emotional competencies that impact performance and behavior.

Correspondingly, emotional intelligence frameworks enable us to differentiate between emotions and emotional intelligence. Emotions can be considered as an inherent state of the mind that builds from the current environment, history, and contexts. The source of emotions includes circumstances, environment, and knowledge including relationships and moods. An individual's emotions are impacted by his or her feelings and experiences. Emotional intelligence is the skill, ability, and awareness to acknowledge, comprehend, and no particular feelings, emotions, and moods including applying them in a positive way. Learning how to manage feelings and emotions and apply that information to act and behave as well as making decisions, self-management, addressing your problems and leading others.

When evaluating the framework of emotional intelligence it is important to acknowledge that whereas the concept of emotional intelligence may seem a straightforward undertaking, it is not. The ability framework is treated as new intelligence and is limited to the standard criteria for all new intelligence. The ability framework scores emotional perception through taking into account the facial expression, voices, body language and pictures among others. Through emotional perception, you can recognize the emotions of others. Perceiving emotions is assumed to be a fundamental concept of emotional intelligence since it is important to complete any of the other requisite processes used in the ability framework.

Exercise
  a. Choose any aspect of the emotional intelligence framework and critique it

High and low emotional intelligence

The best way to differentiate high and low emotional intelligence is to present the attributes of each. A person with high emotional intelligence will express his or her feelings clearly and directly with three-word sentences such as "I feel like..." With high emotional intelligence, a person will not mask thoughts as feelings. When you have high emotional intelligence, you will not be afraid to manifest your feelings. Most importantly is that a person with high emotional intelligence will not be dominated by negative emotions. For instance, you will not be dominated by negative emotions such as guilt, shame, worry, obligation, powerlessness or embarrassment.

Additionally, an individual with high emotional intelligence reads nonverbal communication with ease. With high emotional intelligence, you will guide your feelings to precipitate healthy choices and reality. Persons that can balance feelings with logic, reason, and reality have high emotional intelligence. With high emotional intelligence, you will cat out of desire as opposed to acting due to force, duty, or obligation. With high emotional intelligence, you will be independent, morally autonomous and self-reliant. A person who is intrinsically motivated has high emotional intelligence. If an individual that is not motivated by wealth, power, fame, status or approval has attributes of emotional intelligence.

Furthermore, if you have high emotional intelligence then you are emotionally resilient. The other attributes of high emotional intelligence include feeling optimistic but also realistic and can allow certain levels of pessimism. With high emotional intelligence, an individual will not internalize failure. The competence of being interested in other people's feelings and being comfortable talking about feelings is considered part of high emotional intelligence. If a person is not immobilized by worry then the person is likely to have high emotional intelligence. The ability to identify multiple concurrent feelings helps build high emotional intelligence.

On the other hand, attributes of low emotional intelligence include not taking accountability for your feelings by blaming other people or the context. If one cannot explain how and why they are feeling then it is a sign of low emotional intelligence. A person with low emotional intelligence attempts to analyze you when you manifest your feelings. Such people start sentences with "I think you..." The messages of a person with low emotional intelligence tend to start with I think you should..." Individuals with low emotional intelligence will lay guilt trips on someone else. Another trait of low emotional intelligence is the tendency to withhold information about how one feels which emotional dishonesty is. If one has low emotional intelligence then he or she will minimize or exaggerate feelings.

Correspondingly, persons with low emotional intelligence will allow things to simmer until they blow up including reacting strongly to things that are relatively minor. Lacking integrity and a sense of conscience is a sign of low emotional intelligence. If one holds grudges and is unforgiving then the individual is showing attributes of low emotional intelligence. Expectedly, a person with low emotional intelligence is uncomfortable to be around. Such individuals act their emotions rather than expressing them out. When one is insensitive to how others feel including playing games by being evasive then it is a telling sign of low emotional intelligence. By having low emotional intelligence your compassion and empathy will be significantly low.

Similarly, low emotional intelligence can manifest as rigidity where the person is inflexible and needs rules and structure to feel assured. When one is not emotionally present and gives little opportunity to emotional intimacy then the person is exhibiting low emotional intelligence. An individual with low emotional intelligence will not take into account the feelings of others before acting. Another illustration of low emotional intelligence concerns an individual that is insecure and defensive and has difficulties to acknowledge mistakes as well as express remorse sincerely. Most individuals with low emotional intelligence cite the lack of other options to the way they reacted and behaved.

Equally important is that a low emotional intelligence individual will show a biased and stereotyped view of everything with persistent negative emotions. Such people might be excessively pessimistic and may invalidate the joy of others. Sometimes, persons with low emotional intelligence may be overly optimistic to the extent of being unrealistic and invalidate legitimate fears of others. If a person feels disappointed, inadequate, bitter, victimized or resentful then the person is likely to be exhibiting low emotional intelligence. Another illustration of low emotional intelligence is when the individual fixates himself into certain paths against common sense or makes a turn at the first instance of turmoil. When an individual seeks substitute relationships with pets and plants including imaginary beings and avoids connections with people than the person may be having low emotional intelligence.

By the same measure, low emotional intelligence will manifest as being clingy to your beliefs due to feeling insecure and avoiding embracing new concepts and views. A person with low emotional intelligence will describe the details of an event and what they think about it but will avoid telling you how they feel about it. Poor listeners that interrupt or invalidate others might be suffering from low emotional intelligence. The other attributes of low emotional intelligence include missing the emotions being expressed, focusing on facts as opposed to feelings.

Exercise

a. For one to be regarded as having a low emotional intelligence or a high emotional intelligence then the attributes suggested above have to be consistent and not just spontaneous attributes. Using the suggested attributed, describe a classmate or former classmate whom you classify as likely to have the low emotional intelligence or high emotional intelligence.

b. Look for a quiet place and review your actions over the last one to two weeks. Take out a piece of paper or a word processor application and label yourself "Candidate X". Rate the emotional intelligence of Candidate X as either high or low. State the characteristics of the settled on the classification of either low or high emotional intelligence.

Why developing emotional intelligence is crucial

Building emotional intelligence is important as emotions impact cognitive processes. For instance, one is likely to avoid taking the risk if he or she is feeling anxious. The feeling of anxiety makes one perceive the current environment as uncertain and avoiding risk is welcome when an individual feels unsure. Using this knowledge of emotions, intelligent traders will acknowledge that they will be risk-averse when they feel unsettled while traders with lower emotional intelligent might not be conscious of this effect. The illustration above suggests that high emotional intelligence may increase life success chances compared to low emotional intelligence. In overall, emotional intelligence influences cognitive processes and ultimately mediates or moderates our actions at the workplace and at home.

Notably, emotional intelligence can be used to harness emotions to inform cognitive activities and work out problems. The assertion here is that with requisite levels of emotional intelligence one can customize their cognitive activities to the situation at hand. Think of an individual that elicits thoughts of negative outcomes as a way of motivating performance at the workplace. Absolute control of emotions as well as generating corresponding emotions when they are not there to impact the cognitive processes will occur in persons with high emotional intelligence. On the other hand, with low emotional intelligence, it is difficult to trigger requisite emotions to influence the cognitive processes to enhance actual delivery at the workplace or any other context.

At a personal level still, emotional intelligence will enable you to understand your emotions. Through understanding your emotions you will get the power to handle the emotions. By having adequate attention to your thoughts and feelings it will become easier to manage your emotions. Handling your emotions frees you from volatile emotional reaction situations. An emotional outburst usurps most of your mental energy as well as physical energy. Through emotional intelligence, you will learn to slow down reaction to events and emotions and begin to discriminate your reactions to each situation. All of these developments will boost your self-confidence and assertiveness in life when you learn to handle your emotions.

Expectedly, emotional intelligence will make you understand yourself by discovering the specific areas that you need to improve. You can only work on your weakness if you understand the areas you are having difficulties at first. Fortunately, emotional intelligence includes self-awareness which is the process through which one comprehends herself. The competence that allows you to acknowledge emotions that you perceive is part of emotional awareness competencies. An example is where a student self-evaluates and realizes that he is too unease when receiving any form of negative feedback such as being reprimanded or being rejected by the opposite sex.

Another importance of developing emotional intelligence is that it enables an individual to understand emotion language. The ability to correctly acknowledge relations between emotions and words and place verbal labels to the individual and others' emotions is integral of emotional intelligence. There are individuals gifted with the ability to use the correct vocabulary that matches the emotional needs of the context. Such people realize when they are embarrassed and are likely to express how they feel using a requisite term. Even though it seems as another discussion on effective communication, the ability to understand emotion language goes beyond the standard demands of effective communication. In this case, the communicator deliberates seeks to understand the emotion the words used will elicit and also freely expresses his or her feelings during delivery.

Perhaps the best illustration of emotional intelligence can be found when the late former United Nations Secretary-General Koffi Annan lead negotiation in Kenya when the country was experiencing post-election violence that almost turned into national civil war. Each of the antagonizing sides was emotionally charged and repeatedly attempted to derail the mindset of the late Koffi Annan. As a lead mediator, the late Koffi Annan managed to maintain calmness and sought to listen to each side by acknowledging their frustrations and other emotions while also allowing his emotions to manifest but under control. Emotional intelligence increases your ability to remain calm in an emotionally charged environment and this gives you more control and value.

By learning emotional intelligence one learns to employ requisite emotion regulation strategies. Earlier on we suggested that understanding your emotions are important but that might not help if you cannot deploy ways to manage the identified emotions. Fortunately, emotional intelligence covers strategies for handling particular emotions. Think of when you realize that you become emotional when receiving negative feedback in public. Now that you know your weakness, you will need a matching strategy to handle that emotion. Through emotional intelligence competencies such self-awareness, social skills, and anger management you will learn how to safely express the negative emotion.

Exercise

a. In your own understanding, state three ways that makes developing emotional intelligence important at a personal level.

Self and relationship management

For emphasis, you can only relate well with others if you can relate well with your inner self. Good relationship management should begin with inner self and extend to the external space. Focusing on the self, emotional intelligence influences your actions and thoughts as it is self-reinforcing. Think of when you are angry and bang the table, after some time you think again about the unsolved situation that made you bang the table and might walk away in protest or feel emotionally and physically drained. All these feelings and actions reinforce each other extending the cycle. It takes emotional intelligence to break or manage this cycle.

When one has requisite levels of emotional intelligence, he or she will improve the manner in which you handle or identify the emotions including the matching reaction to feelings of others. When one becomes emotionally stable, he or she starts to grow and gain an extensive comprehension of which we are and this enables us to communicate better than others. It is only possible to sustain a stronger relationship with others when we have requisite emotional intelligence levels. For instance, practice capturing how you feel and try to link to how you express it. It is important that you let your emotions manifest as opposed to locking up the emotions.

With good individual emotional intelligence, you will start working on your social skills which improve relationship management. When interacting with people you have to become aware of your emotions and reactions as well as those of others. The process of attending to your emotional need as well as acknowledging the emotional needs of others is a critical part of relationship management. Each person in a group wants to be where he or she is accommodated and respected. All of these needs are highly perceptual meaning body language, diction and tone of communication, as well as actions, impact the relationship in a big way. Think of narrating to your supervisor that you were unwell and the supervisor is busy typing listening to music.

Another important aspect of self and relationship management is how to handle assertiveness. Being assertive does not imply being domineering but simply making your position known and seeking others to acknowledge and respect it. Assertiveness in a relationship can be a source of friction when either of the parties does not acknowledge the concept of assertiveness. Think of an individual trying to assert his opinion and the other person misconstruing that to mean that the former's opinion has to prevail at whatever cost. Fortunately, emotional intelligence enables one to perceive the reactions of the other person and take into consideration when asserting his or her views.

Similarly, being aware of how you behave constitutes part of self and relationship management. If you are not aware of your actions then you are not aware of how they impact others. In a relationship framework, one must always think of how your individual actions will affect others. Through emotional intelligence, learn to notice and note your behavior. With practice, try to note the particular feeling and the matching reaction that you express. The intent of this element in operationalizing emotional intelligence is to become aware of your emotions and how you react to them to have better management of them. Your individual emotions will impact the relationship with others.

Another issue that may affect self and relationships concerns recognizing and discarding ingrained stereotypes and bias. If we become honest, we have ingrained stereotypes and biases against certain religions, races, sexes and places and this subtly manifest in our emotional reaction and communication including behaviors. It is important that one learns to interrogate his or her opinions as a form of self-evaluation to notice any form of stereotype and bias. An emotional reaction that exhibits elements of bias or stereotypes will significantly strain your relationship with others as your weaknesses with respect to emotional intelligence will be perceived as intentional even when they are not.

Last but not least, become accountable to one and to others. Taking responsibility for your emotions, reactions and corresponding actions are critical in building honest and sustainable relationships. One must learn to be accountable to self before expressing accountability in a group setting. Think of a colleague that spoke rudely to a customer but the offending colleague does not want to account for the negative feedback that the customer gave and now the whole sales team that day is left to shoulder the blame of an individual. Without a doubt, all this will strain the relationship in that sales team.

Exercise

a. The author makes an assertion that a good relationship can only happen when each individual works on their emotional intelligence. Do you agree or disagree with this assertion? Why or Why not?

b. Give your own experience of how the self and relationship management worked or did not work.

Emotional intelligence in the workplace

Predictably, emotional intelligence counts at the workplace in several ways. One of the ways that emotional intelligence impacts businesses are that emotional intelligence can spur improved business decisions. Making decisions involves a series of eliciting information and reasoning it out as a group. Most business decisions are reached through meetings and such meetings require each participant to remain cognizant of their emotions and those of others including their reactions. With an environment that appreciates and respects each member, all members are likely to actively and honestly participate in brainstorming sessions leading to rich, multiple views of the issues at hand. In this manner, emotional intelligence has been applied to making the meeting respectful and accommodating to everyone. The other way that emotional intelligence increases the quality of business decisions is by thinking of how the recipients of the decisions will react and behave and adjusting the final decision accordingly.

Additionally, employees with threshold emotional intelligence are likely to act civil and dignified. Employees that have at least average levels of emotional intelligence are likely to be accommodative, considerate and respectful when interacting with others and the public. Emotional intelligence requires one to determine their weaknesses and act on them in the context of emotional intelligence. When an employee recognizes their ingrained biases and seeks ways to eliminate this bias, they are likely to appear open-minded and this will make it easier to interact with diverse groups. By thinking about how others feel or will feel will enable an employee to adjust the diction and reaction to be sensitive to others. The modern workplace is a diverse environment having different ethnicities, genders, religious affiliations, and sexual orientations which calls for an accommodative workforce.

Equally important is that employees with high emotional intelligence are likely to resolve conflicts with more success compared to those that do not. Conflicts are unavoidable because of the unique nature of human behavior and the human mind. A diverse work environment increases the risk of conflicts. When conflicts occur, employees with emotional intelligence are likely to resolve their conflicts with easy as the competencies of emotional intelligence requires one to think about how others feel. Conflict resolution competencies are also among derived competencies of emotional intelligence. The practice of learning to let go of bias and consider how others feel can significantly deescalate a simmering tension in an organization and all these are applications of competencies of emotional intelligence.

Furthermore, leaders that have high emotional intelligence are likely to manifest greater empathy. Another aspect of emotional intelligence usefulness at workplace concerns the leaders of teams. The actions and reactions of leaders will impact team productivity and eventually the overall productivity of the organization. A leader that has high emotional intelligence is likely to be perceived as empathetic and this is likely to enhance the appeal of the leader to the team. The other importance of having a leader with high emotional intelligence is that the leader is likely to read the impact of new guidelines and changes even before they are implemented and enhance their success.

Correspondingly, employees with high emotional intelligence are likely to reflect, listen, and respond to constructive criticism. For emphasis, employees that exhibit high emotional intelligence are likely to engage in self-reflection, listen keenly, and respond to useful criticism. Self-reflection is critical for continuous employee improvement and in some professionals is directly related to quality such as in the healthcare field. Most individuals have challenges responding to criticism even where such criticism is constructive. Fortunately, emotional intelligence prepares each person to seek and welcome feedback and learn from it. Against this backdrop, employees that exhibit high levels of emotional intelligence are likely to improve by embracing and learning from constructive criticism. In overall, the productivity of the workforce of the organization will improve when its workers exhibit high levels of emotional intelligence.

Some of the ways that employees can enhance their emotional intelligence are through becoming self-aware. An individual should take note of how they are feeling at the instance of the day. Ask yourself how the observed emotions impact your response. It is necessary that you determine your emotions and how they influence your routine activities. Make an assessment of your emotional weaknesses and strengths. For instance, anger is an emotion but how you express or manage it might be a weakness. Against this backdrop, negative emotions are not weaknesses but how one reacts and manages negative emotions such as banging on the table when angry is an emotional weakness. Allowing anger to prolong its manifest on your mind is a weakness.

Exercise

a. Using two to three sentences give an overview of how emotional intelligence impacts workplaces.

b. Why do you think emotional intelligence is critical in a diverse workplace?

Emotional intelligence and relationships

When applied to relationships, emotional intelligence will enhance the value and experience of relationships. One of the ways that emotional intelligence impacts relationships are that it enables the individual to read the emotions of others. As insinuated earlier, healthy relationships flourish when we learn to acknowledge and respect the emotions of others. Recognizing the emotions of others makes them feel we care and that we are connected on so many levels. The competencies of acknowledging the emotions of others constitute emotional intelligence competencies that include self-awareness and emotional regulation among others. Think of being part of a group where the feeling of each member is acknowledged and respected. The members of that team will feel connected and appreciated and will be free with each other.

Secondly, individuals that are emotionally intelligent will listen to understand and manage their individual emotions. Understanding yourself and the other person is integral to emotional intelligence competencies. Learning to listen empathetically allows you to capture the tone and mood of the communication which makes you understand the message deeper. Understanding the message being communicated is vital to recognize how the other person feels and respecting the feeling rather than judging it. However, during active listening, there is a possibility of your emotions getting triggered and this requires one to effectively manage these emotions. Think of listening to a colleague that is complaining about the supervisor not knowing that the supervisor was your classmate. In this illustration, while listening actively, your individual emotions are likely to be activated and it is vital that you manage the emotions.

Thirdly, emotional intelligence will enable you to understand that your thoughts trigger emotions and managing the thoughts helps regulate the emotions. Most individuals overlook the power of their thoughts in triggering emotions and subsequent emotional reactions. Our human emotions are a function of our thoughts and this realization implies that we can control our emotions by managing our thoughts. For every one of us, it is easier to control thoughts before they become emotions. Emotions require a full release to restore balance but with thoughts, we can safely interrupt them without significant harm to the balance of the mind. In this aspect, one must understand his or her thoughts and activate strategies of managing such thoughts before they graduate into emotions. For instance, when you entertain the thought that you are worthless and not valued at the workplace, you are likely to become agitated and withdrawn.

Fourthly, an emotionally intelligent person will acknowledge that there is a link between one's actions and emotional reactions of other people. How we react emotionally influences our actions. The presence of this relationship should motivate us to manage our emotions to improve the way we behave as this impacts others. Using the same example of feeling agitated, you are likely to walk continuously and appear unsettled and are likely not to listen to other people trying to speak to you. Expectedly, such people might either feel that you are ignoring them or that they might notice that you are agitated. Your reaction may continue affecting them as they might avoid bringing a report at your desk or they might informally meet to decipher what is bothering you. The conclusion of this argument is that our individual emotions and actions may have a propagating negative or positive effect on those we relate with.

Fifthly, determine what calms you down and utilize it. When it comes to applying emotional intelligence in a relationship, it is important to discover what works for you and utilize it as often you can. Using the example of agitation, for some people walking helps them drop the anger. For some people when agitated and at home they prefer dancing. The common attribute of what helps you defuse an emotion is that you have to engage in another activity that distracts you from the thoughts and converts the emotional energy into physical energy. In most cases, seeking to convert emotional energy into physical energy will work but unfortunately when this conversation leads to harm then the approach should be unethical at best and criminal at worst.

Sixthly, pay attention to social awareness to enable you to control your thoughts in the long-term. Since we realized that thoughts trigger emotions, the core focus when managing emotions should be on your thoughts. A keen exploration of the issue makes us conclude that the environment influences our thoughts through past experiences, environmental triggers, and context of the situation. For this reason, social awareness is critical in managing thoughts and eventually managing emotions leading to healthy relationships. If you possess social awareness then you have significant control of your thoughts and consequently your emotions.

Exercise

a. The writer makes an interesting assertion that one of the effective ways of managing emotional energy is to convert into physical energy. For instance, when feeling disappointed you can jog around the track to deviate your mind from the negative thought and corresponding emotion. Do you agree? If not, why?

Chapter 2: The Application of Emotional Intelligence

Handling Impulses

A sudden thought or emotion that is overwhelming is known as an impulse. With respect to emotional intelligence, an impulse is an irresistible emotion or urge. Regulating an impulse will involve purposely seeking to increase or lower the intensity of emotion as well as committing not to act on a desire. The requisite skills for managing an impulse include decision and control of where you direct attention to. Recall that our emotions originate from our thoughts and the implication of this revelation is that learning to control our thoughts will lead to improved management of the emotions. You can direct your attention to or away from certain thoughts as a way of handling impulses. Against this backdrop, learning to make a decision and managing where you direct your attention to will lead to improved management of impulses.

Additionally, one should learn to stop the temptation to act on a desire. For this measure, you should develop emotional awareness as well as social awareness. One of the ways to develop emotional awareness is to create a journal of specific emotions and how you reacted to it. With a journal of the frequent emotions and how they manifest, one can develop an intervention that seeks to slow down or stop the trigger factors that cause that emotion. If you feel irritated on certain days and you manage to determine the underlying causes, then it is advisable to manage those factors as opposed to managing the subsequent reaction. The desire is to let out your entire anger manifest while the suggested intervention is to discourage your mind enjoying full control of the emotion. Expectedly, this measure is learned through practice over a considerate period of time.

Furthermore, it is necessary to think about things that calm you when you feel highly emotional. When you feel exhilarated or irritated, it is suggested that deviate your mind to thinks that calm your mind. When activating this intervention, you may have to temporarily depart from the current moment to enable you to take your mind to past experiences that elicit calmness. For instance, you may think of the moment when your favorite team won and you jumped up in celebration and admiration of their resilience when facing a disappointing situation. On the other hand, you might divert your mind to a past experience where you were excited and went on a spending spree leading to difficulties sustaining your routine expenses when feeling exhilarated on receiving a salary increment. The emphasis here is that learn to divert your mind to things that calm when highly excited or irritated.

Correspondingly, it is important to develop adaptability by demonstrating flexibility when facing changing situations is critical in fighting off impulses. Difficulties with managing impulses suggest that the individual has challenges with allowing the mind and body to adjust. Expectedly, allowing impulses is appealing as it is a way of letting your mind and body desires to triumph and cost least mental energy initially. Fortunately, by learning to be adaptable by embracing flexibility in thoughts and actions will increase your competencies of handling impulses. For instance, instead of always of expressing your anger due to feeling disappointed you can accept that sometimes one must be ridiculed. Once you add some room of alternative outcome and reaction to a specific emotion then you can safely exit the emotional meltdown through selecting the least adverse action.

It is also necessary that you develop a set of values that helps checks your desires. It is important that one develops a set of values and principles that guides the individual in any situation. In essence, when one has a set of values, he or she is simply trying to train the mind to learn to act in a certain manner that might be against the impulses. For instance, if one of your values is to remain calm in any situation then you are explicitly training your mind to accept disappointments and process the anger in a civil manner. Against this backdrop, developing a set of values helps demarcate the limit of your impulses and sets the path to developing emotional awareness and self-regulation.

Exercise

a. List any three impulses that you face or have faced.

b. Suggest ways that you can increase management of these impulses through emotional intelligence competencies.

c. In earlier segments of the book, the author encouraged the expression of emotions by arguing that emotions are a form of energy and it must be dissipated to help restore the emotional balance of the mind. However, under this segment, the author is suggesting that one should control impulses. The main reason for this argument is that impulses are unique aspects of emotions as you temporarily lose any form of control of the emotion. Do you agree with this assertion? Why or why not?

Handling difficulties and setbacks

Difficulty situations will always exist because at one point we are taking risks as well as the fact that there are external factors beyond our control. One of the effective ways of handling setbacks is to select the situation by avoiding circumstances that activate adverse emotions. For instance, if you feel irritated when a deadline is fast approaching then it is suggested that you start planning and working earlier by splitting the work into modules. You can go further and inform your colleagues that short deadlines may make you react adversely. Where possible, change the environment to get away from triggers especially where the triggers are not human entities. If you are under pressure to complete a task then a noisy environment may aggravate your emotional reaction to the situation. Changing the environment or seeking to eliminate noise, in this case, might improve your handling of the approaching deadline.

Secondly, learn to adapt to the situation. The main qualification for vouching for modifying the situation stems from the realization that we cannot always control every situation. For situations we cannot control, learning to adjust to the situation is helpful to avoid a negative emotional reaction. For instance, if you are fired from work, it is important that you do not get stuck fighting the disappointment forever. It would help if you adjust your mind and lifestyle to the new status of an unemployed person. With the adjustment, it becomes much easier to start rebuilding your ambitions and your life. Individuals that are unable to learn and unlearn might have difficulties adjusting to situations which increases the likelihood of adverse emotional reactions. However, they are some situations where even individuals with high emotional intelligence might have difficulties adjusting such as grieving or divorce.

It is also important that you learn to redirect your focus. It is human to want to excel and be counted among the influential people. For this reason, our minds tend to focus on our ambitions or what we consider as the ideal life. The continued burden on the mind to process only positive news and desires increases the uneasiness and inability to acknowledge and process negative feedback in routine interactions. For example, you competed in a sports activity and your team was bundled out. All team members feel disappointed but you are also angry at one of the team members who reported for training late and you feel he could have performed better. Each time you let your mind wander on the possibilities that your ream would be having been it not for that one member your negative emotions aggravates.

Related to the previous strategies in handling setbacks is changing your thoughts. As indicated earlier on, thoughts impact emotions and eventually the emotional reaction. While it appears easy, changing thoughts might be a challenge on its account. Changing thoughts requires letting the mind let go of something it is trying to resolve. Fortunately, using cognitive reappraisal you can replace adverse thoughts with constructive thoughts. Additionally, by learning to relax the mind you increase your abilities to navigate difficult situations. There is a possibility that sticking to negative thoughts might be related to self-esteem issues but everyone tends to grapple with negative thoughts as a way of resolving a challenging situation. With good practice, you will learn to drop negative thoughts by replacing them with positive ones.

Sometimes everything might fail and in that case, emotional regulation is the best measure. In this strategy, an individual focuses on managing the emotions that are manifesting. For instance, you are unable to prevent an episode of anger so you focus on handling the simmering anger by walking away, going to the washroom, playing music or informing the other person to take a break because you are irritated.

Some people manage anger by sitting down, changing facial expressions or walking down the stairs than up. For emphasis, emotional regulation can be for both positive and negative emotions. Being highly excited can make it difficult to continue with a conversation of discussion and you should think of how winners of music awards or lotteries behave. Think of someone that cannot stop laughing when everyone else is sad.

Exercise

a. Collins works in one of the leading exporters of spectacles. Due to the nature of the products the company has a strict work routine as well as a strict work routine. Collins is the supervisor of a team of 14 people. When the team fails to process orders on time and the client is issuing threats of canceling the order, Collins become anxious, agitated and sometimes almost abusive. From this narrative identify the challenging situation? Assuming that delays with processing cannot be completely eliminated, how can Collins improve his reaction to setbacks? How can employees working under Collins improve how they handle the challenging situation which is a boss that might not understand they are not to blame?

Handling stress and anxiety

First, identify the origin of the stress. Like with any problem, you can only develop an effective solution when you understand the trigger of your stress. Even though it appears a straightforward endeavor it is not. Some of the major stressors include moving, changing jobs, going through a divorce or increased workload either at home or workplace. One of the areas that contribute to stress and that we overlook is our individual thoughts, behaviors, and feelings that increase routine stress levels. For instance, it might not the job that is stressing but fear of not delivering on that job. An effective strategy to determine the source of anxiety is to keep a journal of the emotion and the corresponding reaction. From the personal journal of your emotions, you will get an opportunity to evaluate your anxiety and the triggers.

Secondly, accept that you have stress and anxiety. The second major step in managing stress is to acknowledge that you have it. Most individuals with stress and anxiety rarely accept that they have the condition until late. Part of this reluctance of accepting stress and anxiety is because it is portrayed as a form of mental weakness and an inability to cope with demanding situations. All these stereotypes package one as not employable because all workplaces have demanding situations. However, stress and anxiety is not a weakness but an acknowledgment of your body that it has reached the known limit which is specific to each individual. For this reason, one should learn to determine their individual stress levels as they differ per individual and they are not a weakness but an affirmation that your body feedback loop is working.

Thirdly, recognize and accept your role in creating stress and anxiety. Another flaw in handling stress and anxiety is when we blame situations and people other than ourselves. The truth is that we participate in precipitating stress and anxiety. For instance, if you fail to plan for work during peak season at your workplaces chances are that you are going to face heightened workload within a short period of time. If you fail to adequately participate in social moments then chances are that you are likely to bottle up emotions that might precipitate anxiety. When you acknowledge the role you play in creating the stress and anxiety then you will commit to enhancing that role to precipitate positive outcomes with respect to anxiety management.

Fourthly, even with these measures, it is still important that you maintain a stress journal. The purpose of the stress journal is to help you identify routine triggers of stress in your life and the manner that you intervene. You are likely to realize that in most cases, you rarely intervene to these stressors or you consistently apply ineffective interventions. The other purpose of a stress journal is to help you develop a long-term effective intervention plan after determining the nature of the triggers of stress and how you normally react to the stress. While this suggestion appears easy to implement, most people do not always feel motivated to write down one of their challenging moments but with multiple attempts, you will manage to keep a stress journal.

Additionally, one should avoid unnecessary stress and anxiety. After identifying the sources of stress in your life, you are likely to acknowledge that not all of these sources are necessary. For instance, being overly worried about your productivity at the workplace is not necessary if you plan and understand your job tasks well. If you learn to let go of thoughts of disappointment and accept that we all cannot attain the same level at the same time, you will start focusing on the positive aspects of your life. If you define your limits and assert them then some of the pressures that you invite can be eased. Indeed, stress is not completely avoidable but not all stress is necessary. For instance, you can choose to avoid people that wear you out emotionally.

Last but not least, manage your environment. The environment contributes a significant part of your stress and anxiety but it can be managed to a limited extent. For example, if evening news makes you edgy you can turn off the TV. If traffic makes you agitated, you can leave the house earlier than you normally do or use a different route. Another way of managing the environmental factors that trigger stress is to list to-do-list and how you will accomplish the action and what happens when you cannot. In essence, you are giving an action plan as well as a contingency plan.

Exercise

a. Sometimes it is difficult to prevent a stressful situation. In this case, one should consider altering the situation to increase chances of defusing anxiety or stress. From your past experience, list any two moments where you felt stress that you could not navigate through and how you finally overcame it.

In the workplace

Indeed emotional intelligence is critical at the workplace in multiple ways. One of the ways that emotional intelligence is useful in the workplace is to help each one of us understand our emotions and how they affect others. There are a number of people that do not recognize their emotions and this makes difficult for them to manage them as well as acknowledge how their reactions impact others. Fortunately, emotional intelligence can help an employee acknowledge their emotions and seek to exercise self-regulation to avoid making their emotions a liability. Workplaces are increasingly becoming diverse and it is important that we acknowledge our emotions and how manifesting they will impact people of other ethnicities, gender, sexual orientation, and different faiths. For instance, if you are angry and express that anger when speaking to a minority group they might interpret your emotional reaction as belittling them or their efforts.

Additionally, emotional intelligence enables employees to build social skills. Employees mostly work with others and the public. Emotional intelligence is a fundamental of social intelligence. Employees use emotional intelligence to visualize how the other person is feeling and adjust the communication to be considerate yet effective. In the absence of emotional intelligence, an employee would not care much about how the other person is feeling and effectively lack social skills. It can be argued that possessing high emotional intelligence predisposes one to high social skills that are admired at workplaces. Think of a high qualified engineer that is regarded as temperamental and most workers avoid engaging him on challenging issues. Workplaces are modularized and each category of employees must effortlessly interact with others in the organization.

Furthermore, emotional intelligence can help employees understand their actions to customers and the public at large. When employees understand how the public will feel then they will act in a manner that is considerate. Think of an employee that understands that developing an ineffective solution will irritate the customer; such an employee is likely to diligently work to offer an effective solution to customers. At the forefront employees that have high emotional intelligence are likely to relate well with customers by listening empathetically and speaking with consideration. From these illustrations, emotional intelligence helps humanize employee actions which give the organization a human face. Think of the businesses that handle you with respect and appear keen to listen and act on your feedback.

Another importance of emotional intelligence is that it can help improve routine communication. Employees are forever entangled in grapevine communication at workplaces. It is during this form of communication that some employees feel unease or offended by their colleagues. The uneasiness can easily spiral into entrenched dislikes of each other and affect productivity. However, with emotional intelligence, all employees learn to read the feelings of others and even predict how their colleague will react to certain communication. Using emotional intelligence, the communicator will adjust or stop the communication if it makes others unease. Think of one of your colleagues making fun of Muslims not knowing that your in-laws are Muslims and wondering why you seem disinterested in the joke.

For leaders, emotional intelligence can help leaders cultivate their empathy attribute. A leader with high levels of emotional intelligence is likely to be perceived as a listening and approachable leader. An empathetic leader listens to the emotions of the audience and pays attention to the emotional value of the communication. Simply put, a leader with high emotional intelligence is a listening leader and members of the team are likely to feel valued in such a setup. Now think of a leader who cares not about how others feel when communicating. The members of such a team are likely to feel undervalued and demotivated. The advantage of having a motivated team is that there is less need for supervision and employee turnover is low.

Equally important is that emotional intelligence is critical to solving conflicts. As indicated earlier on, conflicts are unavoidable at workplaces. With increased diversity at the workplace, the frequency of conflicts will only increase. Fortunately, with emotional intelligence that explores self-regulation, emotional awareness and social skills the communication of each employee to the other is likely to be considerate. Each time employees disagree, they are likely to see the justification for the disagreement as opposed to precipitating a crisis. Manifesting emotions in a diverse workplace can aggravate conflicts as the communication and actions may be misinterpreted as entrenching discrimination. Emotional intelligence is a critical means to defuse tensions before they graduate into conflicts.

Exercise

a. Emotional intelligence is widely applied at the workplace, to enhance interactions among employees, to improve the relationship of the organization and clients, to increase the effectiveness of a leader, and to help defuse conflicts. Pick one of these areas and describe how emotional intelligence can help improve workplace environment or organization's human face.

Coping with trauma

Trauma arises when one goes through a disturbing event and feels overwhelmed. For instance, near-death injury and torture can trigger trauma. Trauma should be acknowledged and viewed as an acute stress event. Like any mental health issue, the first step to manage it is to accept that it is present. A number of affected people might not accept that they are suffering from trauma or the might not understand that they have trauma. The initial step to coping with trauma is to help the individual acknowledge that they are suffering from trauma. As suggested earlier, most people have a negative view of any mental health as it is seen as having a weakness. It is important to underscore that trauma is a way of the mind forcing you to seek closure from a disturbing experience to restore balance.

Secondly, note the triggers that worsen relapse of the intense fear that you experience. For instance being left alone, avoidance of loud noise and being startled by sudden movements. Just like stress and anxiety, trauma has triggers that we should identify. For instance, if you were shot at in a noisy environment then each time you hear or walk into a noisy environment your mind will work you through the past gruesome event. It is important to understand that your mind is trying to protect from harm by activating the extreme reaction you exhibited when your life your threat. In this manner, coping with trauma is a way of minimizing the gruesome memory to allow your mind to stop treating any minor disturbance as a potentially grave threat to your life.

Thirdly, note your reactions each time you relive the traumatic experience such as lack of sleep, guilt, withdrawing to oneself, and anger. With time you will notice that you react differently to each trigger of your trauma. For instance, you might physically lock up your environment each time you hear movements outside. Other people might inadvertently scream when a car suddenly breaks. Try to write down each trigger and your reaction. For instance, you might write "Movements outside-I hurriedly closed the door and kept quiet". Using the example above, the trigger for reliving trauma was movements outside and your reactions were closing the door. By maintaining a journal of triggers and how you reacted, you will have adequate information to help design an intervention to manage trauma.

Fourthly, design a plan to handle the emotional reactions. Before working on the underlying cause, it is important to handle the emotional manifestations as they can be a danger to oneself and others. It is important to design an intervention plan to manage the reaction due to triggers as some of the reaction can pose danger to yourself and others. Think of each time you hear a bang your instinct is to jump due to past gruesome experience with a lone gunman. A person with this reaction can harm himself if standing near a balcony or any other place where impulse movement can pose danger. An immediate intervention plan should focus on degrading the intensity of the reaction of a person suffering from trauma.

Fifthly, design an intervention to handle the underlying traumatic event. For a long-term solution, it is important to address the underlying cause. Start by letting the person drop the self-blame for predisposing himself or herself to the way of harm. It takes time for victims of trauma to drop self-blame. The temptation for self-blame by the victim is to enable them not embark on the journey of seeking justice that reminds them of the circumstances that led to the gruesome experience and aggravate the self-blame. Sometimes it might be necessary to visit or recreate the event to help the individual walk the mind through the situation several times to gain mental stamina. In other cases, it might require extracting the individual from the physical environment to eliminate physical reminders of the unfortunate incident.

Lastly, confront situations linked to traumatic events gradually but exhaustively. While it is important to address the underlying factors that led to trauma, it is also important to address other issues that relate to the unfortunate event. For instance, assume that Richard was assaulted by armed robbers in his house, one week after moving in a new neighborhood. After addressing the circumstances directly related to the unfortunate incident it is also important to tackle other issues that might have precipitated the incident including those that Richard has no control over. For instance, Richard highly social nature that includes inviting fresh acquaintances and posting about his house furnishings on social media. Care should be exercised when confronting situations that caused the traumatic events so as not to appear to be judging the event.

Exercise

a. Recall any movie that depicts a traumatic event of a lead character. How did the lead character react or cope with the situation?

b. Search the Internet and read about survivors of 9/11 terror attacks in the United States are coping with the trauma.

Coping with reactions

Coping with emotional reactions concerns how and when to manifest emotions we feel. First, become aware of your emotions. Before managing emotions, you need to understand and acknowledge the emotions by knowing why you are feeling that way. By understanding your emotions you will manage to understand why you react the way you do. For emphasis, most people assume they know or do not need to know their emotions. Without the knowledge that the emotion that you experiencing is anger, you will not appreciate why you shout, walk away or bang the table. In the absence of knowledge of the type of emotions manifesting you will struggle to handle the reaction. Keeping an emotional journal can help one comprehend the frequency and type of emotions manifesting and lead to better coping mechanisms.

Secondly, learn to safely express your emotions. Emotions are a form of energy and locking them up will not help. Learning to safely express your emotions is important. For instance, the author suggested that the best way to handle emotions is to convert the emotions into physical energy from emotional energy. In this manner, when your anger starts building, you can start dancing, wash your face continuously or take a walk. However, in reality, you will not always get an opportunity to convert emotional energy into physical energy and these calls for other ways to manage emotional reactions. One of the ways to attain coping to a reaction is to anticipate the emotion and define the reaction including the limit of that reaction.

Thirdly, seek feedback and improve. Like with any learning process, you need to seek feedback about your emotional intelligence and commit to learning. For instance, you can ask colleagues to rate your temper. When asking for feedback it is important not to view the information given as profiling you. The colleagues are simply giving you information based on the way you interact with them. If your colleagues say you are temperamental do not pin them down or justify your temper. The intent of getting feedback is to get the views of other people and look for ways to remedy the suggested shortcomings. Using the information solicited use emotional intelligence to work on your weak areas that include not feeling interested in the conversation of others.

Fourthly, develop multiple options and weigh on which one is beneficial. Most people do not realize that they have a choice when it comes to emotional reactions. For instance, you do not need to reply to every statement made against you. Sometimes you just need to acknowledge that your personality and your delivery are different though related. By criticizing your output does not necessarily mean that they are criticizing the whole you. When facing backlash for the work you did, you can choose to process the feedback as judging your delivery or personality. If you take this into account, you will realize that you do not need to react the way you do in most circumstances. Additionally, you can choose to substitute anger with a positive feeling.

Fifthly, learn to unlearn. One of the overlooked competencies is the ability to unlearn. Most people can learn but cannot unlearn. The ability to unlearn allows you to restructure thoughts, emotions, and reactions. High coping levels are likely to manifest in individuals that unlearn. Our emotional reactions are impulsive and it takes a mental effort to drop convenience of manifesting our feelings. Expectedly, shouting or crying when angry will make you feel at peace but it is not the most appropriate reactions when working with people. Coping with reactions should not be misconstrued to mean bottling up emotions but rather safely expressing emotions by being considerate to others. The intent of this strategy is to urge you to unlearn impulsive reaction to negative emotions such as screaming or banging the table.

Finally, account for your reactions. It is important you become for the reactions you show to your emotions. By being accountable to your reactions you will appreciate their value and burden and seek to maximize their good value and minimize their cost. An emotional reaction has value and cost. When you are angry and shout at others, the value of the reaction is that it quickly dissipates your anger and the cost of the reaction is that you appear volatile and other people will be uneasy being around you. Most people blame situations or other things rather than taking up responsibilities to the way they reacted.

Exercise

a. How do you handle disappointment when alone?

b. Similarly, how do you handle disappointment when with people?

Chapter 3: Recognizing Emotions

Common and negative emotions in the workplace

Envy

One of the common workplace emotions is envy and the emotion is allowed to manifest as each one of us admires to be accomplished. It is allowed for human beings to nurse and pursue ambitions routinely. However, when one becomes uneasy with the achievement of others to the point of being affected mentally and physically then the feeling is envy. Like any other mental condition, persons that are envious rarely accept that they have a negative emotion. Envy is likely to affect the workplace negatively. Even though a limited and occasional form of envy is welcome as a necessary trigger to improve and strive, if it becomes unmanaged it becomes an adverse emotion. Since workplaces appraise their employees, individual employees are likely to admire to accomplish more like their feted colleagues and this can breed feelings of envy.

Correspondingly, one of the ways of recognizing a feeling of envy is when you persistently feel that you deserved the reward bestowed on your colleagues. Even though workplace systems might not always play fair, in most cases they closely capture the natural setup of the organization and individual as well as group contributions. It is expected for some employees especially the lowly rated ones in terms of productivity or personality to feel unease with the ranking system at the organization. However, the feeling of resentment becomes envy when one persistently feels that he or she deserved the reward and not the current winners of the reward. If it becomes difficult to let go of this feeling for days to months then you are probably envious and this will negatively affect your delivery at the workplace.

Additionally, when one entertains the thoughts of working underhand to upset the candidate who appears accomplished at the workplace then envious feelings are manifesting. If unmanaged, envy can push an individual to scheme to degrade the performance of celebrated colleagues at the workplace. Think of a jealous employee that seeks to sabotage the work that was left unsaved by a colleague celebrated as a highly accomplished worker. In extreme circumstances, envy can lead to unwarranted disagreements and attempts to have the targeted accomplished colleague fired or face disciplinary action. Take the case of Janet who is envious of the achievements of Mark at the workplace and manages to find Mark's computer on and open. She then manages to use the log in the email of Mark to send pranks to several colleagues without the knowledge of Mark. In this case, the intention of Janet is to malign Mark because she is envious of him.

If each time you interact or work with certain colleagues, that are recognized at the workplace and you feel a sense of jealousy when you are likely envious of their achievement. Sometimes envy might appear as jealousy which means you feel heightened suspicion of your colleagues. Take the case of Janet who views everything Mark suggests with suspicion. In the mind of Janet, all suggestions of Mark are meant to make him flourish at the workplace and for this reason; she doubts and questions every suggestion of Mark. So far Mark has been restrained but he is starting to notice that Janet might have a general disliking of his personality. Like any other feeling, a limited and infrequent manifestation of envy is welcome but when it persists then it becomes a liability to the individual and the entire organization.

On the extreme scale, you might incessantly seek to make everyone aware of your contribution when working in a group which is a manifestation of envy.

Sometimes envy is expressed with incessant attempts to seek validation. When envy is unmanaged an individual might seek to broadcast his or her every contribution in each task to attract attention to their productivity value in the group and indeed the entire organization. The reason for such individuals broadcasting their contribution to the team is to explicitly nominate their self for rewards. In other words, unjustified completion at the workplace can be a form of envy. Such kind of envy might make the affected individual make unjustified communication in the form of reports and send them to the supervisor of teammates.

Lastly, an individual with envy might embark on unplanned career development including seeking more workload than necessary. Envy is related to uncontrolled desire to excel and persons with envy might enroll for evening or weekend classes to enhance their career for the sake of attracting recognition and other forms of reward. Such individuals might also work extra hours or do more work than they should in the belief that they will be recognized. For this reason, if you feel the urge to engage in unplanned career development and work extra hours to attract recognition and other rewards from your organization then you are probably envious. The major effect of envy is that it clouds your objective thinking and fixates your mind to particular things and people denying you the full experience.

Exercise

a. Give three situations in the recent past where you felt envious.

b. How did you overcome the envy?

c. What are the effects of envy that you experienced?

Worry or nervousness

Another common feeling at the workplace that is regarded as negative is feeling nervous or worried. For emphasis, feeling nervous is a welcomed as it is part of human feelings but like any emotion regarded as negative, it should be handled way to avoid creating an adverse impact on work relations and output. One of the ways you will notice when feeling nervous is that you become restless. If feeling worried, your mind is stuck on what could possibly go wrong and this elicits fear especially the worst case scenarios that replay on your mind. Expectedly, you will try to elicit multiple courses of action within a short period of time which only makes you more unease to the point that your uneasiness manifests in actions.

For emphasis, when feeling worried your mind wanders on the possible worst outcomes of the situation that is disturbing you. When worried you imagine the worst and rarely see the immense possibilities present. Think of being worried that your work contract might not be renewed. From this illustration, you are likely to feel nervous and start thinking of worst cases only where you are unable to pay house rent, service loans and kids and your wife are looking at you with huge disappointment. You are likely to be thinking of losing your social class and probably end up on the streets. Therefore, when one gets fixated on worst-case outcomes within a short period of time there are chances that he or she might be worried.

Thirdly, when feeling nervous you might want to excuse yourself from a meeting or conversation to be alone. One of the noticeable effects of being worried is that you might want a few minutes alone to recollect your mind and think through the situation objectively. If you get nervous in a meeting or during a conversation you might excuse yourself to go to the washroom or go back to your office cabin to calm yourself before resuming. For this reason, when you get the urge to be alone during a conversation or a meeting there are chances that you are feeling nervousness. Take the case of Grace who received a text that a foreclosure notice had been placed on her house while just about to start attending a meeting at work. She became sweaty and her heart pounded first and she did not trust how she would react so she excused herself and rushed to the washroom to think through the issue.

Fourthly, with a feeling of worry, you will talk to yourself or talk to objects to listen and assure you. When feeling worried, you are likely to talk to inanimate objects or engage in soliloquy to help you let out and think through the situation disturbing you. When an individual starts talking to himself or herself then chances are that the person is feeling worried. Like any other emotion, feeling worried is necessary to alert your mind and prepare it for any eventuality. However, the feeling becomes a concern when it begins overwhelming you or frequently recurs which will affect your productivity and relations.

Fifthly, when feeling nervous your nonverbal communication will give you away from such as trembling voice and avoiding eye contact. Another way of noticing nervousness is to pay attention to nonverbal communication that exhibits what a person might be masking. For instance, one might say that he or she is okay when the face is sweating, and the voice is trembling. The voice pitch of an individual who is nervous is likely to be high or low rather than the accustomed pitch. The gestures of an individual that is nervous are likely to be misaligned to their verbal message even though they are trying to project themselves as being in control of the situation. An individual that is worried might pace up and down frequently than he or she usually does.

Lastly when nervous you are likely to become self-conscious that everybody is aware you are unsettled and feel that they are judging you. In most cases, when one is nervous you are mentally aware of the state and try to compensate for the nervousness. As earlier on indicated, the society ridicules negative emotions forcing people to feel ashamed of manifesting such emotions and nervousness is one of the emotions. Feeling anxious is not the desired emotion and one is likely to feel that the audience or colleagues have noticed the negative emotions and are having a low opinion of the person.

Exercise

a. How do you handle nervousness when addressing an audience?

b. Why do you think society ridicules negative emotions instead of acknowledging them and seeking to safely express them?

Anger or aggravation

Anger might be one of the commonest negative emotions at the workplace and this is expected.

Workplaces have targets and evaluate their workers which create pressure and deadlines. When workers are under pressure and where the value is judged by defined expectations then they are likely to act under pressure. When one is pushed to the limit by deadlines then an individual may react impulsively by clicking, walking away or banging the table. Workers are also evaluated on the contribution to overall productivity and when workers feel the scoring system is not fair then they are likely to feel agitated. Anger can then be acknowledged as a negative emotion when one is unable to satisfy the expectations at an individual and public level.

Secondly, anger manifests as feeling highly offended. The reason for anger frequently manifesting at the workplace is due to the existence of diversity at the workplace where slight misconceptions are treated as deriding and degrading an individual. There are diverse workers in contemporary workplaces such as different sexual orientations, ethnicities, sexes and religious afflictions. What one might regard as normal communication and reaction might be offensive to others. For this reason, most contemporary might find offensive communication that another employee thinks is casual and harmless. Think of Richard who makes jokes that Muslims are oriented to violence without understanding that Ruth finds such casual talk offensive because one of her sons has converted to Islam. Ruth is really irked by the talk of Richard of Islam religion to the point of abandoning the tea break earlier than she does.

Furthermore, anger is exhibited as feeling insulted by the words or actions of a colleague. Another expression of anger is when one feels insulted by the actions or words. Such feeling is not necessarily linked to self-esteem issues rather lack of emotional intelligence by the person communicating. Mark is the leader of a team of five engineers at a local consultancy firm. Recently Mark suggested that nonperformers will be dropped and John felt insulted because he was rated low in the last appraisal. The feeling of being insulted aggravated to the point that John started considering terminating the contract to venture into business. In essence anger as an emotion is manifesting as a feeling of being insulted.

Similarly, anger is shown as feeling locked up by circumstances. When one feels that they have no options then it could be anger manifesting. If you are denied options or feel that you are not allowed alternatives then you will feel that you are under pressure. You will feel neglected and this form of anger. When you feel chained to processes that you have no control over you are likely to react by retreating to yourself or engaging in unjustified arguments. If you left with fewer options you are likely to feel cornered and undervalued. Restricted options might be misinterpreted to mean that you are not trusted and you are likely to feel insecure and scream at people at the slightest provocation.

Another way that anger is expressed is in the form of frustrations. When one feels the inability to control situations then anger is an expression of that frustration. As suggested when you feel cornered you are likely to feel no need to continue anymore. With frustrations, you will start disregarding the laid down procedures or become disconnected from your work. Feeling defeated will demotivate you and lead to a casual and unproductive approach to working. The other impact of frustration as a form of expressing anger is that you are likely to blame situations and other people rather than being accountable to yourself. In extreme circumstances, a frustrated employee might suggest that he or she does not care and mishandle customers especially when handling complaints.

Lastly, anger is manifested as sensitivity to negative feedback. The other form that anger manifests at the workplace is when one becomes sensitive to communication and actions. An individual that feels frustrated and undervalued by situations might become highly sensitive to the slightest hint of doubt or negative feedback. Such individuals quickly activate defensive mechanism by exploiting the conversation to play the victim card. When a person expresses anger as sensitivity to communication, he or she will invoke race, gender, sexual orientation, and religious affiliation to suggest that they are being discriminated against. The intent of being sensitive is to lock out others from fully exploring the issue at hand. In most cases, anger is an internal development and few people want to accept that they need help to enhance their emotional coping which makes sense as a way of locking up any conversation on the reaction.

Exercise
a. Anger is one of the common and negative emotions in the workplace. How do you cope with anger?

Dislike

Dislike is one of the negative emotions that is overlooked and sometimes misinterpreted to be something else. In this context, dislike refers to the general and unjustified feeling of disassociating and disinterest in someone or something. At one point you might have disliked someone or some movie character without any reason for feeling that. Dislike needs no justification just like love. Some dislikes are driven by social bias that eventually reinforces your personal bias. For instance, you might have just disliked the new worker even before you met or interacted. When you try to look for the reasons for disliking the innocent you do not get any. Dislike is a risk to developing social relationships as it denies you objectively assessing other individuals and this will affect your productivity as well as theirs.

Secondly, dislike manifests as stereotypes. Another way that dislikes manifests is in the form of stereotypes. If you have stereotypes against Latinos then you do not need any reason to dislike them, you only need to see or be told that the new colleague is a Latino. If you have stereotypes against women at the workplace then you only to meet one to dislike her. It is also important to acknowledge that you might develop stereotypes at the workplace even if you did not have one initially. Some of the dislikes are due to generalization. For instance, you might dislike the new intern from the University of Texas simply because the previous from the institution failed you at the workplace. For this reason, you do not need any reason to dislike the new interns as you have already developed a stereotype against the mentioned university.

Thirdly, dislike expresses as isolation. The other way that people express dislike is by isolating their targeted victims. Avoidance of meeting and involving the person you disregard is a way of expressing the feeling of dislike. The victim of the dislike might or might not notice the dislike. From this illustration, dislike costs mental energy as well as the overall productivity of the organization. If you harbor a dislike for an individual then you are likely to manipulate the composition of a team to push the individual away without taking into account the overall needs of the organization. Think of a new hire who is one of the few competent engineers in the new certification system but you dislike the new hire. You then go ahead and isolate the individual costing the organization of production.

Fourthly, dislike may manifest as a superiority complex. If you allow feelings of dislike to flourish then at some point you are likely to feel like the ultimate validation entity of what is good and what is not. The exhibition of feeling more important than others propagates dislike as a feeling. Essentially superiority complex is a contradiction of the intent of emotional intelligence competencies that seeks to advocate for consideration. In this manner, dislike is a confirmation of the likely low emotional intelligence of an individual. Take the example of Haron who feels that he is more qualified than everyone else at their company and feels that he understands better who should be hired and promoted. The company that Haron works for has promoted a colleague that Haron feels that the candidate is least qualified according to his sentiments but the organization thinks otherwise. While Haron is not jealous, he generally dislikes people he thinks are not up to his qualifications.

Fifthly, dislike may occur as justification. Sometimes dislike manifests as a justification. For instance, an employee may dislike another to justify his internal feelings. One might dislike others so as to feel valued and influential. Some people might show dislike to make other people seek to make peace with them which makes such individuals feel they matter. In a way, some people exercise dislike to help precipitate a crisis that enables them to exercise self-validation. For example, Richard dislikes Kevin but the goal of this behavior is to make Kevin seek ways to make peace with Richard. By having Kevin recognize that he needs to get along with Richard, the later feels valued in the organization.

Lastly, dislike can manifest as judgment. In some cases, the dislike of someone occurs due to the subjective judgment of the individual. When you judge someone by the first appearance as well as including any disability or physical features that you rate lowly then this is a judgment-driven dislike. The judgment of individuals is largely informed by stereotypes and past experiences. In judging people subjectively you classify them mentally and handle them based on that classification.

Exercise

a. Using initials only, list some of the people you dislike but cannot explain why you dislike them?

b. Which politician do you generally dislike; you have no reason for the feeling of dislike?

Disappointment or unhappiness

Disappointment like anger is a common negative feeling at the workplace. Feeling disappointed is unavoidable at the workplace due to needing to accomplish targets or fit in a certain circle. When a good intentioned worker fails to reach the set target or attain average score during appraisal then the person is likely to feel unhappy. The feeling is initially welcome as it can motivate the person to self-evaluate and commit to delivering more in the next cycle. Unfortunately, the feeling of being disappointed can persist and cause adverse effect to the self-esteem of the individual including negatively affecting the social life of the person. When you continuously feel disappointment you are also likely to express anger which might negatively affect your relationship with others.

Secondly, disappointment manifests as feeling let down. When one feels unhappy then the person is likely to feel betrayed by others. In most cases, disappointment arises when your expectations are not met and this can make you blame others for what happened. Think of an employee that was in a group and the entire group member contracts have been renewed except the one for the disappointed employee. Such a person is likely to lay blame on situations or other people for his unhappiness. Blaming others can lead to a new social problem especially where the person blames part of his family for disappointment at work. Think of an individual whose contract was not renewed but the person blames his wife for not being supportive enough during the period he was under probation which can create marital issues.

Thirdly, disappointment expresses as feeling not as good as others. When one is disappointed when the person is likely to feel inferior to others especially where others have excelled. Think of an employee whose contract was not renewed but those of others in the group were renewed. Such an employee is likely to feel that he or she is not as good as the others despite reassurances from the team. The reason for feeling inferior is that when one feels unhappy he or she is likely to blame oneself other than objectively navigating the circumstances that led to feeling unhappy. Remember our example, where only one member of the group failed to secure a new contract while others sailed through and the individual ended up blaming himself for the new status.

Fourthly, disappointment can manifest as not feeling appreciated enough at the workplace. As expected, if one is disappointed when the person might feel that his or her input is undervalued at the organization. It is difficult for a disappointed person to believe that the outcome was due to internal and external factors and not necessarily personal culpability. Finding somewhere to lay the blame is a way for your mind to reach some closure and restore mental status balance. Unfortunately, most people find it convenient to blame themselves other than identifying the factors that precipitated the disappointment. It is important that we unlearn the trained way of handling disappointment by learning not to blame ourselves for disappointment always.

Fifthly, the feeling of disappointment can show as avoidance. In some circumstances, disappointment might express as isolation where an individual that does not feel happy retreats to his or her world. Such a person might feel that by being alone, he or she will get time to reflect and design new strategies to improve in the next evaluation cycle. While brief retreat to your world is allowed, it can become problematic when you prolong the avoidance of social moments as this allows the negative emotions to reinforce each other. Think of our example where the single employee whose contract was not renewed in a group withdraws to his world and continues to blame everything including fate and entertains thoughts of quitting employment altogether.

Lastly, disappointment may manifest as increased need for validation. In most cases when one feels disappointed, then he or she might require affirmation that they are still as good as anyone else. Such individuals might engage in frequent submissions of reports or seek frequent feedback not because they want to improve but they want to get adequate positive feedback as a form of validation of their worth in the group. The need for validation is a confirmation that one is feeling disappointment especially in the case of a workplace after an appraisal report feedback. Disappointment in this context affects productivity by making the individual demotivated and engaging in unnecessary activities to help validate his or her worth to recoup from the unhappiness,

Exercise

a. How did you handle disappointment while in college?

b. How did you express your disappointment?

Chapter 4: Improving Emotional Intelligence

Emotional intelligence in the relationship

Notably, emotional intelligence will help each party in a relationship empathize more with one another. Empathy is one of the easily noticeable signs of emotional intelligence and concerns acknowledging and making a priority to the needs of the other person. Empathy is one of the components of a healthy relationship. In a way, empathy advocates for limited self-sacrifice to prioritize the emotional needs of the other party. The perception that the other person is involved in the conversation and is listening increases the feeling that one is valued. However, empathy does not imply that you totally forego your emotional needs in favor of the other party. The emphasis of empathy in a relationship is that it allows you to view the world from the other person's perspective which boosts mutual understanding.

Through emotional intelligence, one can initiate a critical conversation without it escalating. If you are emotionally intelligent then you are likely to process criticism safely. In a relationship, constructive criticism is necessary and it helps propagate the relationship. However, when criticism is not well received then it can shut down routine communication. Lack of communication is a significant danger to any relationship. Emotional intelligence can help prepare an individual to negative feedback and such a person is likely to be receptive to criticism. Some people are likely to react to criticism with anger and feeling judged. An individual with high emotional intelligence will welcome criticism with the understanding that emotional intelligence levels can be elevated to fix some of the shortcomings raised. Criticism in this context is treated as an avenue to recognize, learn and understand more your emotions and your actions.

Another criticality of emotional intelligence in a relationship is that it enables the parties to be fully vulnerable with one another. Being fully vulnerable to one another enables you to connect with one another. Most people are uneasy with being vulnerable to other people save for the one they trust. Emotional intelligence allows you to express your emotions fully including the negative emotions that you might not freely express in public. With emotional intelligence, you will acknowledge what holds you back including understanding how and when to manifest the emotions. The other partner will easily accommodate your vulnerability and view the world from your eyes due to exercising empathy which is a competence of emotional intelligence.

Expectedly, emotional intelligence competencies will enable you to express your feelings directly. Lack of emotional intelligence will force one of the partners to use passive aggression or silence to handle a conflict. Fortunately, emotional intelligence can help any aggrieved partner to explicitly express their feelings as well as be assertive. The understanding that all emotions are inevitable and should be expressed is enough to motivate one to manifest his or her emotions. In a context of emotional intelligence, all parties can manage to exercise empathy and this should make communication on issue direct. In this manner, emotional intelligence is a component of operationalizing honest in a relationship. Think of Janet who is feeling angry at Mark for not picking her calls all day and is confident that Mark understands why she is agitated. On the other hand, Mark empathizes with the way Janet is feeling and understands that the disappointment by Jane is not judging Mark and he does not take things personally.

Equally important is that emotional intelligence can help you apologize to each other and restore normalcy. One component of emotional intelligence is recognizing your emotions and being accountable. If each one of you acknowledges their emotions and assumes full responsibility for participating in the creation of that emotion and the subsequent reaction then it becomes easier to offer apologies when you offend the other. Another way that emotional intelligence can increase understanding by offering an apology is when an individual acknowledges and processes feedback from the other person. Emotional intelligence advocates for seeking views of other people about your emotions and corresponding reactions and utilizing the feedback to improve. Offering an apology is a way of acting on self-feedback and feedback from the other people in a relationship.

Lastly, emotional intelligence can help partners in a relationship recognize and solve a conflict. As indicated earlier on, conflicts are unavoidable due to each one of having different sets of values, views, and approaches to routine issues. With the increased diversity in relationships, conflicts are bound to happen frequently as well as due to increasing pressures of life such as high cost of living. With emotional intelligence, resolving conflicts becomes more practical as each party is willing to drop their hardline stance and process the issue from the viewpoint of the other party. If empathy flourishes, then the feuding parties are likely to soften hard stances and emphasis more on shared understanding enabling them to work towards a solution.

Exercise

a. In your previous relationship (friendship, work or romance) what caused the final disconnect according to you?

b. How could you have used emotional intelligence to resuscitate the failed relationship above?

Body language

Expectedly, body language is a critical part of emotional intelligence as it impacts empathy. Think of a colleague saying that he feels sorry for what you went through while smiling. Let us start with facial expressions as a form of nonverbal communication. Take note that the human face is highly expressive and can communicate countless emotions without verbalizing anything. Additionally, facial expressions tend to be universal unlike other forms of nonverbal communication. For instance, facial expressions for sadness, happiness, and fear tend to be universal. Most aspects of nonverbal communication are involuntary but with some coaching and practice, one can increase the alignment of facial expressions and verbal communication. At home, you can use a webcam to record random speech to see if the facial expressions and verbal communication. You can also try speaking about different emotions in front of the mirror to evaluate how your facial expressions align with your verbal expressions.

Another aspect of body language to watch out for is body movement and posture. Understand that people perceive you differently depending on the way you walk, stand or sit. For instance, if you are pacing up frequently while speaking to an audience then there are chances that you are hurrying the conversation or are feeling unease. Standing or leaning while listening or speaking shows that you are likely feeling tired or disinterested in the exchange. Slumping on the chair shows that you are feeling tired, distracted or disinterested in the conversation. If you are speaking to someone then the person is walking away then you are likely to view the person as showing rudeness or disinterest. Fortunately, body movement and posture as a form of nonverbal communication is highly controllable compared say to facial expressions.

Furthermore, gestures impact what you are communicating. The way you move your hands during communication constitutes gestures. Think of when you signal your friend to shut up, come or stop. When speaking with someone, the movement of your hands is sending their individual messages and you should try to align that message to what you are verbalizing.

Compared to body postures, gestures are not easily manageable as they involuntary reactions. Fortunately, through practice, one can improve the alignment of appropriate gestures and the intended messages. For example, when you throw up your hands in the air with quick succession while speaking, there is likelihood that you are offended. When you point using one of your fingers there is likelihood that you have judged the individual.

Similarly, eye contact is a critical aspect of nonverbal communication. Maintaining eye contact is critical to make the other person feel that you are interested in and are participating in the conversation. While keeping eye contact shows that you are actively participating in the conversation, sustained eye contact for more than one minute will distort the message as it amounts to staring or judging the individual. When speaking to an audience it is important to move your eye contact across the audience to avoid narrowing the nonverbal communication. Even though eye contact is nonverbal communication, it is important to acknowledge that some individuals were born shy and their lack of eye contact should not be misinterpreted to mean that they are disinterested or timid.

Additionally touch is a form of nonverbal communication. Even touch is not widely used but it is a form of nonverbal communication. Firm but gentle touch shows safety and care and this might be necessary for a romantic relationship and in parenting. The other common form of touch in public communication is a handshake. A firm handshake communicates confidence while a handshake that is not firm may communicate a lack of self-confidence. It is important to note that not all societies and individuals prefer handshakes. Even though handshake is a form of nonverbal communication, some people are born with medical conditions that make it difficult for them to shake hands such as an excessive palmar sweating condition known as hyperhidrosis. When processing handshake or lack of handshake allows some room for exceptions.

Then there is space which is a type of nonverbal communication. The physical distance between you and the other party in the communication is referred to as space. When you move very close to the other person, he or she might feel uncomfortable. However, for parties in a romantic relationship being closer physically might be the desired form of communication on some occasions. At the same time being significantly far from the person, you are communicating might suggest disinterest or casualness of the message. Being unnecessarily far from the person that you are communicating with might also increase distractions in communication. Think of when you are attending a workshop forum where the speaker sometimes moves close to your direction and goes back and stands at a distance that most people feel comfortable to listen.

Lastly, there is a voice as a form of nonverbal communication. The pitch of the voice communicates nonverbally. When the pitch of a voice is raised you are likely to process the message as anger or disappointment. An average level pitch will suggest that the speaker is settled and the emotional value of the message is within known limits. Similarly, a low pitch may suggest a lack of confidence, sorrow or discomfort of the speaker. However, it is important to understand that sometimes adjusting the tone is necessary to break the monotony, emphasize or show transition when communicating.

Exercise

a. How does tone affect the intent of communication?

b. Gestures and facial expression are among the most difficult forms of nonverbal communication to control. Do you agree with this assertion? Why or why not?

Active listening

Start by paying attention to the speaker and the message. Effective listening requires being in the mind and differentiating the message. Within an audience or any context of communication, there are multiple messages and exchanges and the ones that are needed are regarded as noise. For instance, people moving up and down, the wind blowing hard and phones ringing are communications but that which is regarded as noise. For this reason, an individual practicing active listening should selectively listen by focusing only on the speaker and the message conveyed. The other form of noise is internal and this includes diversionary thoughts and getting distracted by other thoughts. Think of feeling the urge to check social media updates while listening which is a form of internal distraction or noise.

Then show that you are listening through your body language and gestures. Communication is simultaneous and two-way and it is important that you reciprocate your listenership by expressing appropriate body language with respect to how the message is affecting you. Remember that the lead communicator relies on your reaction to adjust the communication for the benefit of everyone. For this reason, not communicating back is denying the speaker an early assessment of his delivery and the impact of his message. When listening actively, nod, clap and move your eye movements to help process the message and increase your focus on the communication. Think of revival churches' audiences' reaction to fiery preaching. Such audiences raise their hands, smile and nod actively.

Correspondingly, give feedback. One way of providing feedback is to politely interrupt and let the speaker repeat or capture your concern. The other way of giving feedback is to use nonverbal communication to make the speaker understand that you are receiving or not getting the intended messages. However, in most cases when one is not listening actively the feedback is involuntary such as slumping in the chair, staring at the roof or feeling disconnected from the audience and the moment. Some of the feedback constitutes bad listenership behavior such as seeking clarification from a colleague while the speaker is busy speaking. Both negative and positive feedback can be safely expressed using nonverbal communication.

It is important that you note down questions or areas that need clarification to avoid distracting your listenership. One of the issues that affect effective listenership is when an individual requires clarification and cannot get a chance to interrupt the speaker. For this reason, the individual allows the pending question to stay on the mind while timing for an opportunity to pose it to the speaker and this affects effective listening. One of the best ways to accommodate the need for clarification while effectively listening is to note down the question or area you need clarification and continue listening. By capturing the question on your notebook, you will free your mind and allow it to focus on developing communication.

Additionally, summarize what you listened. As you listen summarize the key points which allow your mind to internalize and connect the developing message. Noting the main points also helps you become mentally alert by connecting your body to the moment. While communicating, noise is everywhere in the form of colleagues whispering, phones vibrating, flickering lights and internal thoughts that deviate you from the message. Making an internal summary as well as a physical summary on your notebook or journal you increase your levels of concentration. However, it is important to understand that writing too much will affect effective listening. The goal is not to summarize but to listen and that is where you should focus.

Where possible, change position to get a clear projection of what is being spoken. Sometimes you might have to change your position where possible to get a clear view and voice projection of the speaker. Physical distance affects the efficacy of communication, especially where the audience is large and the projectors are absent. However, modern technology has improved large audience communication by using electronic projectors and sound public address systems to make voice projection and visualization of the speaker available at any angle. It is also not advisable to change seats during a speech as this might create unnecessary realignments and noise that might interrupt the speaker. A good practice is to arrive early enough or reserve a seat that will place you at a comfortable angle to receive and process the message from the speaker.

Exercise
a. How do you maintain attention when listening when having the urge to use your phone?

Mindfulness and relaxation techniques

There are six common mindfulness and relaxation techniques that are widely applied and one of them the breath focus. It is a simple but powerful technique where you take a long, gradual and deep breaths referred to as belly breathing. While breathing, try to gently disengage your mind from sensation and thoughts that distract you. The breath focus technique might useful for individuals with eating disorders to enable them to concentrate on their bodies in a positive way. Caution should be exercised for individuals with health-related breathing difficulties such as heart failure and respiratory elements. The technique of breath focus works by helping distract your mind from other thoughts and activities and this makes the mind perform a less costly task of breathing which helps ease your muscles and mind.

Additionally, there is another technique known as the body scan. In this technique, we mix breath focus with gradual muscle relaxation. Start with a few minutes of deep breathing then concentrate on one aspect of your body at a time and release any physical tension mentally. The value of body scan technology is that it can enhance mind-body connection awareness. Individuals that might find this technique useful are those from recent surgery and are grappling with body image issues. The body scan technique can be done independently or in a group setting. Additionally, the body scan technique can be accomplished by having an instructor guide you through the entire exercise. For this reason, this technique is highly flexible and costs less in terms of resources including time.

Another mindfulness and relaxation technique is guided imagery where one conjures up soothing places, scenes or encounters to help relax and focus. Fortunately, they are multiple applications on guided imagery. One of the impacts of guided imagery is that it can help reinforce a positive vision. The major weakness of guided imagery is that it can be challenging for persons having intrusive thoughts or persons that find it difficult to conjure up mental images. A suggestion of guided imagery is to visualize a staircase colored with all the rainbow colors and then walk or sit on each differently colored step. Then allow your mind to associate that color with positive natural sightings such as a lush green garden for the green colored step on the staircase. Using this repetitive and simple task, your mind will eventually delink from current costly thoughts and engage in this relaxing exercise.

Equally important, there is mindfulness meditation as a technique of mindfulness and relaxation. In this technique, one sits comfortably and concentrates on breathing as well as inviting your attention to the mind to the current moment. Our minds tend to wander into the past or future to help create continuity. Mindfulness meditation is likely to help individuals with depression, anxiety, and pain. The essence of this technique is to slow down the mind from being preoccupied with the future or the past. The mind controls us but in mindfulness and relaxation techniques we are trying to control it. Like any other form of meditation, one requires a calm place that is free from physical and electronic forms of distractions to successfully engage in mindfulness meditation.

Similarly, yoga is increasingly being used as a mindfulness and relaxation technique. Yoga involves a series of flowing movements where the physical aspects are expected to align with mental focus and distract the individual from continued thoughts. When feeling disturbed, it is a combination of emotional energy and physical energy that reinforce each other or rival each other which wears us out. With yoga, we harness both the physical and mental energy to calm the entire body. The other advantage of yoga is that it can improve flexibility and balance. In this way, yoga not only calms you but also exercise you. However, due to its physical cost to the body, yoga might be unfit for persons with certain health conditions. For this reason, yoga might be unreasonable to persons with pain or health problems that inhibit movements.

Lastly, saying repetitive prayer may help calm and focus the mind. For individuals that are irreligious, one can create a chant that helps the individual feel inner peace and calm. Saying repetitive chants reinforces the message to the mind and makes the mind believe or let go in line with the contents of the chant or prayer. It is important to understand that this technique might not work for everyone for it requires allowing your mind to travel to the message contained in the prayer or chant. One must also conjure up the ideal place or paradise when saying prayer or chant repetitively.

Exercise

a. Choose any two mindfulness and relaxation techniques and explain how you can implement them?

Chapter 5: Emotional Intelligence and Leadership

Good leadership

Emotional intelligence can enhance the honesty and integrity virtues of a leader. Through emotional awareness, a leader will get an opportunity to read his emotions and become aware of how he reacts to the emotions. At the same time, the leader will seek to take into consideration how other people are affected by the emotions of the leader. When communicating with others or when demonstrating something to the team, a leader will try to be as open as possible because he does not want others to feel disappointed by his dishonesty. In this manner, emotional intelligence is among the building components of an honest leader by making the leader aware of how others will react to his communication and actions.

Additionally, emotional intelligence can make a leader influential and inspire others. Through emotional intelligence, a leader will improve his or her communication and listening skills. For instance, emotional intelligence can enhance effective listening through empathy during a conversation. When speaking, a leader will appreciate the emotional value of each sentence and this will enhance the choice of words as well as the tone of speaking. When a leader shows empathy, actively listens, and speaks with consideration then the rest of the team is likely to feel respected and inspired. The other reason for the team likelihood of feeling inspired is to excel and get to display their leadership skills. It can be argued that emotional intelligence humanizes a leader from the viewpoint of those being led.

Furthermore, emotional intelligence can improve the commitment and passion of a leader. When a leader invokes emotional intelligence competencies to help understand the emotional needs of the team then the leader is showing commitment to helping improve the welfare of the employees. The determination to help others get the communication as well as not be affected by your emotions is an expression of passion and commitment to your role as a leader. Think of a leader who does not take critically the effect of his emotions and reactions to the team. Such a leader is likely to be viewed as disconnected to the realities of the workplace needs. Lastly, emotional intelligence allows a leader to get continuous feedback that can help enhance the passion to discharge leadership duties.

Another way that emotional intelligence can build a leader is by making the leader a good communicator.

As expected, effective communication is critical for a leader. Communication is the main avenue via which the leader delivers and receives an exchange of the message. There are nonverbal and verbal forms of communication and all of these forms need to reinforce each other. Communication is a science and art meaning that individually we can improve the communication to satisfy our message exchange needs. An individual that is open minded by dropping personal biases, and welcomes the views of others and at the same time pays attention to the effect of how he is communicating is likely to be effective in communication.

Equally important, is that emotional intelligence competencies improve decision-making capabilities of a leader. Decision-making capabilities require recognizing personal biases, overcoming impulses and regulating emotional reactions. In the absence of emotional intelligence competencies, one is likely to make impulsive and subjective decisions. Such decisions are largely ineffective as they are not based on the complete picture but rather what is convenient to the mind. Fortunately, emotional intelligence competencies resolve most of the shortcomings in decision-making by helping us actively acknowledge and discard stereotypes and ineffective communication. Imagine a leader who is not actively listening to suggestions or feedback during a brainstorming session. Additionally, you need emotional intelligence to effectively read nonverbal communication or nonverbal feedback regarding some of the decisions you want to implement.

Through enhancing the accountability of a leader, emotional intelligence competencies improve the appeal of a leader. For most people, they tend to avoid taking responsibility, especially where negative emotions are involved. Leaders not are tempted to blame situations or others instead of assuming full responsibility for what happened. However, by exhibiting emotional intelligence competencies, a leader will learn to process negative feedback without feeling like he or she has failed. One of the biggest reasons for not taking accountability by leaders and any other person is because it suggests that they are not competent enough to deliver. Stated differently, taking accountability increases chances of processing negative emotions and negative emotions are considered a weakness at the workplace.

Exercise
   a. In your own words, how does emotional intelligence and leadership connect?

Adaptation

One way that emotional intelligence can enhance leadership is through enhancing the flexibility of an individual during crisis situations. Leaders need to be adaptable because they cannot always control everything, especially external environment factors. High emotional intelligence implies that a leader is open-minded and can take different viewpoints other than the conventional one. Crises are unpredictable and require leaders to be open-minded. For example, through emotional intelligence, a leader will try to view the situation from the victims' perspective, from the organization's perspective, and from a personal viewpoint. Additionally, during a crisis, a leader will learn to process the volatile emotions from the victims as a way of expressing their anger and not necessarily to discount the leadership of the organization.

Secondly, managing work stress by invoking emotional intelligence can improve the influence of a leader. A leader has to guide the rest of the organization to new thinking and acting that the rest of the team might find difficult. If the leader is the only one adapting then the flexibility of the leader might not yield much. For this reason, a leader has to persuade others and dissuade fears of the team when trying new viewpoints and processes. A leader must convince others to trust his moves and this requires emotional intelligence. Persuading people requires one to understand their fears and this can be required empathizing with them including active listening.

Thirdly, emotional intelligence can enhance innovative solutions when handling problems. Part of being flexible requires thinking and acting creatively as some new circumstances require unconventional solutions. The ability to improvise is important for a leader. Take a case where a leader is rigid and this slows down the entire organization. Inflexibility might be a suggestion that a leader has a fixated mind which may correlate with persons that harbor and exercise stereotypes. Adaptability and creativity are likely to correlate with open-mindedness and this is a competence of practicing emotional intelligence. By taking into account different views of others as well as a personal view, a leader is likely to generate a creative solution.

Fourthly, emotional intelligence can enable a leader to handle unpredictable situations with significant success. One of the benefits of emotional intelligence competencies is that it can improve our anticipation and processing of negative emotions. One of the uneasiness with change and uncertainty is due to the fear of the unknown. Organizations have to take varied forms of risks such as embracing new technology, increasing affirmative action, and adjusting the business model. We all fear failure, stagnating, legal consequences and loss of status and for these reasons, human beings prefer status quo irrespective of its value. With emotional intelligence, one is likely to open up and welcome the possibility of negative emotions. In other terms, emotional intelligence is likely to make a leader a risk taker.

Fifthly, emotional intelligence can increase the adaptability of a leader by activating interpersonal competencies. Part of being adaptable as a person requires you to relate with others and this makes interpersonal competencies highly critical. A leader needs to disrupt the status quo and create a new equilibrium. During change, people are uneasy and emotional and it requires fine interpersonal skills to navigate the volatile environment and defuse tensions. Leaders must develop interpersonal skills which are essentially social skills. If you can recall, social skills are a derivative of emotional intelligence and a leader with social skills will exhibit effective interpersonal skills.

Lastly, emotional competence can enhance cultural adaptability of an individual. In the current workplace and the world, diversity is ever increasing and leaders require the flexibility of the mind. Leaders with emotional intelligence are likely to recognize and respect other cultures. While acknowledging and respecting other cultures appears easy, it is not easily implemented. Like most human beings, leaders are likely to view the world from the way they were raised which unfortunately includes stereotypes and personal biases. For this reason, a leader has to unlearn in order to become culturally competent. Most workplaces now have diverse workers in terms of ethnicity, religious affiliation, and gender among others. Our upbringing impacts the way we process issues to do with diversity and in grapevine communication, all people struggle to remain culturally sensitive.

Exercise
  a. Luke is the team leader of engineers at Redline Consultancy, a startup that offers customization of cars. The company wants to change its current information system and this might necessitate retraining the employees as well as a reshuffling of employees. Using the adaptability competencies influenced by emotional intelligence, suggest three ways in which Luke can show effective leadership at the organization.

Leadership and performance

Through emotional intelligence leaders will acknowledge the impact of culture on productivity. Firstly, it is important that leaders connect leadership and performance of employees and indeed the organization. With good leadership, employees are likely to feel motivated and show commitment to the organization. One way of ensuring good leadership is to be an emphatic leader who listens and appreciates the team. A leader has to take the position of those he is addressing to understand their reaction and needs. The other way that emotional intelligence can help a leader make workers feel valued is social skills where a leader excels in interpersonal skills and leaves employees feeling respected and valued.

Additionally, motivated employees are likely to deliver. As indicated above, employees that feel valued are likely to attain set targets. Each one of us wants to value that we count and leaders play a significant role in making the team feel they matter. A leader needs to address the workers as a critical part of the organization and make it clear that the role of the leader is to occasionally refocus the energy of the team. Using communication techniques, the leader will help the employees feel they belong to the organization and when employees treat the organization like theirs, they tend to become accountable.

Furthermore, emotional intelligence application can help prevent conflicts in the workplace. Conflicts are unavoidable at the workplace. In the absence of leadership, conflicts will escalate and might lead to sabotage, employee turnover and in extreme cases violence. Leaders with emotional competencies will apply conflict resolution strategies to defuse tensions and restore normalcy. Good leaders will help individual workers gain and exercise emotional competencies and help lower chances of prolonging disagreements into conflicts. Without high emotional intelligence, leaders would inadvertently aggravate conflicts by appearing impartial or judgmental. For this reason, emotional intelligence enables the leader to defuse conflicts and sustain productivity in the workplace.

Through emotional intelligence, employees are likely to feel accommodated and deliver. Contemporary workplaces are increasingly becoming sensitive and leaders have to ensure that all workers feel safe, appreciated and accommodated. One of the common causes of leverage and friction is diversity. What one employee might consider as casual talk might turn out to be insensitive to the other employee. As the areas of diversity increase, so is the sensitivity of employees to verbal and nonverbal communication. The common areas of diversity include sexual orientation, gender, ethnicity, and religious affiliation. A leader is able to navigate the emotive issues and help employees understand their diversity and make everyone feel respected at the workplace.

Equally, important leadership helps make the team adaptable. Performance of an organization is also determined by how flexible the team is. Think of a team in an organization that is rigid and take significant time to adjust to the new business model or the newly installed system. The time spent to adjust costs the organization productivity. Good leadership ensures that the workers are flexible to ideas and approaches. The quality of flexibility is critical in helping the organization capitalize on changes in the market, especially technological changes. The leader is critical in helping shape the minds of the team in embracing changes at the organization.

For emphasis, good leadership helps communicate clearly the goals of the organization. Communication of targets and the ultimate goal is important to influence the attitudes and behaviors of the employees. A good leader will invoke emotional intelligence to ensure that the message communicated clearly. One of the ways of ensuring that the team understands the message is to employ empathetic speaking and active listening. It is also important the leader acknowledges the emotional value of words when communicating. Ineffective communication implies that the employees might not be having a shared understanding of the needs of the organization.

Finally, leadership helps elicit and act on feedback. Another critical element of productivity is extracting and acting on feedback and leadership offers an opportunity to capture passive and active feedback. There is always the feedback generated by the system but it is important to capture the qualitative feedback from the team itself concerning how they feel about the leader or the organization system. With this feedback, the leader should adjust communication and approach to maximize productivity in the organization. It is one of the overlooked areas in leadership and some leaders are not at ease with handling negative feedback. However, feedback is a critical aspect of continuous improvement.

Exercise
a. In your opinion, how does leadership relate to organizational performance?

The six styles of leadership

The first style of leadership is the visionary style and it concerns mobilizing people towards a vision. The visionary style works well when there is a clear direction or where change is required. For this reason, the visionary style of leadership is good where the climate is positive. The emphasis of visionary leadership is not reaching the specified place but rather getting everyone to embrace the vision. Another aspect of visionary leadership is that it advocates for autonomy and enables people to innovate and experiment to attain the set goal. In practice, failure when implementing visionary leadership is accommodated and employees feel comfortable experimenting in ways of moving the mission forward. It is important to have a clear mission that all employees acknowledge before attempting the visionary leadership style.

Secondly, coaching leadership style is another approach to leadership. The coaching style of leadership involves training employees to become better at what they do. It is important to acknowledge that there is a difference between coaching and micromanaging. The role of the manager in this leadership approach is to help employees evolve in their role and challenge the employees to surpass their assumed capabilities. In this approach to leadership, the manager grants employee's advice, tools, and support they require enabling them to succeed. However, coaching does not imply that the leader dictates what an individual will do at each step but instead directs them to attain the improved version of themselves.

Thirdly, there is the affiliative leader where the manager acts as an affiliate and makes connections in the entire organization. The intent of the affiliative style of leadership is to create a harmonious work environment where each employee knows and works well with each other. Expectedly, employees will not always get along and will disagree but this style of leadership seeks to fix that. The affiliate leader mends any broken trust in the organization. A leader can become an affiliative leader by developing a culture of recognition on the team. By building trust, the group will become closer and this will help build relationships.

Fourthly, democratic leadership is another common style of leadership. With the democratic leadership style, a manager will align a group towards an outcome. Democratic style of leadership is employed where the manager is not fully certain on the direction that the organization should take and the leader wants to leverage off the views and beliefs of the crowd to develop a clear path. The democratic style of leadership is critical when handling big decisions that might impact the future of the business. The motivation of the democratic style of leadership is the realization that collective intelligence is superior to individual knowledge.

Fifthly, there is a pacesetting leadership style. In this approach to leadership, the leader defines goals attainable without taking into account the feelings of the team. Pacesetting leadership places pressure on the team and exemplify what is required of the team. As expected, the pacesetting style of leadership has the risk of derailing the team and should be used with caution. It should be applied temporarily and for a short period. Sometimes a company has to expect much from its employees irrespective of the needs of workers and one of such situations include when the company is handling a crisis. One of the ways to attain results using this style is to balance this style with recognition.

Lastly, there is a commanding leadership style. In this approach to leadership, the leader invokes fear. The commanding style of leadership creates a perception of emotionless and cold. In most cases, the commanding leadership style evokes extreme negative effects on the culture of the company and is highly ineffective. The commanding style of leadership might only qualify during crises and it is not the best approach to show leadership during such times. The overall recommendation is to avoid using a commanding leadership style. For this reason, avoid ordering your team around and instead inspire participation as well as clearly explain the full situation. In conclusion, it is important to accept that there is no universal style of leadership and you might have to blend different styles of leadership depending on the situation you are facing. It is important to remember that you do not have to accomplish everything alone just because you are a leader as the team can always help with ideas. Empower your team to become leaders on their account and lastly develop emotional intelligence.

Exercise

a. Critique the commanding style of leadership.

b. Critique visionary leadership style.

How to improve

Start by recognizing the efforts of your team individually and collectively as a way of motivating the team. Acknowledging the contribution of your team is critical as it makes them feel valued and interested in group activities. Recognizing the contribution of your team is a form of reward and assurance that workers.

Some leaders might overlook the criticality of recognition as it is a psychological need. The recognition does not have to be formal always. For instance, you can offer positive remarks each time a team member submits a complete report on time. You can also use gestures or facial expressions to show satisfaction with the work of a team member. A leader has to show that he or she appreciates the effort of the team to make them feel they count.

Secondly, inform the team that the expectations are temporary and as a team, it is the ideal time to work together. When executing the command style of leadership or pacesetting style of leadership it is necessary that you furnish your team that the huge expectations are temporary to enable them to adjust and accept mentally the new demanding schedules. Sometimes a leader might be forced to hurry everyone especially during a crisis and under such circumstances; the leader might not allow democracy including understanding. In other terms, the leader might show less emotional intelligence competence when the sustainability of the organization is at stake. Under such circumstances, the leader has a duty to notify the workers why the environment has suddenly become stiff and burdensome to enhance their understanding and acceptability of the new approach of doing things.

Ensure to share the results of the efforts of the team on the bigger picture. In a typical organization, workers operate in a modularized manner. If not managed, the workers in each department might not have a comprehensive view of how they link to the entire organization productivity. For instance, the cleaners in an organization might not understand how they impact the success of the information technology department. A leader should seek to help individual teams understand how they collectively impact the entire productivity of the organization. For instance, cleaners ensure that the information technology department is organized and operate on time in a clean environment. The information technology department directly impacts the rest of the department.

Additionally, learn to trust your employees and improve your communication skills to enable you to freely discuss issues with anyone on the team. Without showing trust in your employees they will feel undervalued or they will feel that they are highly replaceable. If you trust your employees they will feel the urge to act responsibly as they are relied on to act independently. The absence of trust will make employees wait for supervision and deliver just enough to fulfill the contractual obligation. Trusting employees will also make them feel that they are part of the organization and are likely to take time to think of ways that they can help the organization improve.

Furthermore, offer suggestions to start a discussion on the project. Workers are sometimes reluctant to initiate a conversation, especially where such a discussion might appear to critique the leadership of the company. In such a case, it might help to initiate the conversation as a leader and encourage contribution from the team. In such circumstances effective communication especially aligning nonverbal communication to verbal communication is important. The tone of your voice, your facial expressions and gestures must speak one message to enhance the trust of the team. Before making any decisions, it is important to elicit as many views as possible and the people you are leading might have more effective solutions than you thought.

Lastly, consider all the ideas present and appreciate the contributors. As a leader, you will frequently engage with team members and it is important to acknowledge and appreciate each opinion floated. Leaders that do not appreciate the contribution of each member risk having diminished contribution in the subsequent meetings. Using words such as thank you, noted, appreciated and using nonverbal cues such as nodding, smiling and clapping shows that you are listening and appreciating the contribution of each member present. A leader should make a decision using the best suggestions available but show that he or she has listened and will save the other suggestions for future use.

Exercise
a. Have you ever held a leadership role? If no, think of a movie character that holds a leadership role. How did the leader show growth or improvement in executing his or her mandate?

The five components of emotional intelligence in leadership

The first component is self-awareness and it impacts leadership in several ways. Individuals that are self-aware understand how they feel and have knowledge of how their emotions will impact other people. As a leader having self-awareness implies that you know your strengths and weaknesses as well as portraying as a humble individual. You can operationalize self-awareness in leadership by slowing down your emotional reaction. Imagine if a leader that is quick to react and bang the table when irritated. It would become difficult to disagree with such a leader and one is likely to conform to the demands of such a leader to avoid confrontation. Additionally, self-awareness helps a leader become an effective communicator by understanding how the audience is feeling due to what he or she is communicating.

Secondly, there is self-regulation as an emotional intelligence component in leadership. Each one of us gets the urge to react impulsively as it is the most natural way of expressing and acting on the emotions. Self-regulation relates to the tendency to stay in control and avoid letting emotions guide you. Self-regulation does not imply that one is locking up their emotions rather one is exerting control on the reaction to the emotions. Leaders with self-regulation competency avoid impulse reaction to emotions such as verbal attacks when someone offends them. I will urge to watch the late Koffi Annan who was a former Secretary General of the United Nations and how he handles criticism during meetings or press conferences. Intense emotions and impulse reactions derail the mind of the leader.

Correspondingly, you can enhance your self-regulation through understanding your values. A set of personal rules and personal philosophies constitute personal values. With your individual code of ethics, you will inform your mind of its limits irrespective of the situation. It is also important to hold yourself accountable. The tendency of blaming others is an escapist approach to handling challenges and personal weaknesses. When you assume responsibility for your actions then you are granting yourself a chance to examine and fix your shortcomings. Lastly, it is important to practice staying composed when facing a challenging situation. You can breathe deeply and assure yourself that you will not let the negative emotion overwhelm you.

Thirdly, motivation as a component of emotional intelligence is integral in leadership. Leaders that are self-motivated will work consistently to achieve goals. Such leaders will also show high standards for the work they churn out. One of the ways that one can improve self-motivation is by reexamining the purpose of signing up for the position. Sometimes, people forget what made them take up the opportunity to work and by reflecting on why you took up the opportunity you might reignite your passion for the job. Beginning with what spurred you to assume the role might help you realize the commitment you need to show as a leader.

Then there is empathy as an emotional intelligence element that is expressed in effective leadership. Empathy is one of the critical elements of emotional intelligence and leadership. It is the ability to place yourself in the place of others to understand them better. Leaders with empathy are regarded as understanding, approachable and human compared to those that do not. A leader may show empathy by understanding why the members are unease with the new regulations or why employees are calling for several meetings before they embrace the new changes. With empathy, a leader will not feel disrespected or hated by the team members when communicating newer demanding changes.

For emphasis, contemporary workplaces are striving to be as humane as possible. Leaders that show empathy earn respect and loyalty from the team. When employees speak, try to abandon your position and view the world from the employees' eyes. Being empathetic does not imply that the leader is indecisive. One of the ways of improving empathy is to pay attention to the body language of the speaker and respond to the feelings. Some employees might use nonverbal cues to communicate their fears and disappointments and the leaders must read and respond to these.

Lastly, there are social skills that manifest in leadership. One of the ways of applying social skills in leadership is in conflict resolution. Expectedly, social skills rely on effective communication and active listening. With social skills, a leader will handle and solve conflicts diplomatically. In the absence of social skills, a leader might aggravate conflicts and lead to employee turnover, sabotage and even violence at the workplace. Fortunately, leaders can learn to become polished conflict resolvers and enhance their communication. An emotionally intelligent leader will easily recognize the shared ground of the feuding parties by reading their emotions when certain issues are mentioned and build on the common ground to cultivate a solution.

Exercise
a. Look for one episode of the TV series House of Cards and judge the emotional intelligent competencies of Kevin Spacey? Do you agree or not with his manipulations?

Social skills

One of the skill sets needed for emotional intelligence is survival skills. The specific competencies here include the following guidelines, listening, ignoring distractions and using brave talk as well as rewarding yourself. Social contexts might require you to follow instructions and overlook distractions. Not all people can ignore distractions as the human mind processes everything it can decipher. It is important to train your mind to act in a disciplined manner by avoiding distractions and sticking to the recommended guidelines. It is also important that you reward yourself to enable you to feel worth engaging in social interaction.

The second sets of skills needed in socially competent individuals include interpersonal skills. The particular skills here include asking for permission, sharing, waiting your time, and joining an activity. It takes the experience to know when to interrupt or join a conversation. In most cases, the range of required interpersonal skills depends on the context. The argument here is that the interpersonal skills you exercise when watching your favorite team play are not the same as the one you exhibit when with your colleagues at the workplace.

The third skill sets regarding social skills include problem-solving skills and specifically asking for help, accepting consequences, and apologizing. In social contexts, disagreements will occur and at the same time, the parties in the interaction might require your input to resolve an issue. A socially competent individual needs to identify the underlying causes of the problem, how it is affecting others, why the rest of the people are feeling the way they are, and finally offering impartial and multiple ways of fixing it.

The fourth skill sets include conflict resolution skills and specifically handling loses, accusations, peer pressure, and dealing with flatter. Resolving conflicts is a highly demanded skill in contemporary society that is increasingly diverse. Solving conflicts require being impartial, empathically listening and helping the feuding parties acknowledge their shared ground on the issue. Unresolved conflicts can end social interactions and at workplace affect productivity in several ways. For instance, unresolved conflicts can make some workers quit a certain team or leave the organization altogether.

The fifth aspect of social skills concerns the ability to persuade and influence others. In social contexts, one should possess the ability to convince others. Influencing others relies on emotional intelligence competencies especially empathy and emotional value communication. When you understand the emotional impact of the words in your communication then it becomes easier to use it to win others. Persuading people also means that you appreciate how they feel and take into account when communicating with them.

The sixth sets of skills for the socially competent individual include leadership skills. Within social contexts, sometimes one has to show leadership. Within a group, it will require a leader or a dominant member and possessing leadership skills is part of social skills. A good leader inspires and listens while being visionary. When participating in social contexts, it is important that you cultivate leadership skills and demonstrate them where appropriate. One of the preferred models of leadership is the transformative leadership where the leader motivates the members rather than commanding or setting the pace for the team.

Equally important is communication skills that operationalize social skills. As expected, communication skills are essential in any social activity. Some of the communication skills required includes effective use of nonverbal communication. It is important that the facial expressions and gestures used are appropriate and at the same time tally with the verbal communication. Groups are likely to be diverse and hand gestures might have different connotations for each member involved. For this reason, communication should also include cultural competencies.

Furthermore, building bonds is requisite for social skills. Part of social interactions is developing relationships. Creating a relationship will also require a skill to sustain the relationship. Not all people can initiate and sustain a relationship. The competence of building and sustaining relationships is part of the social skills that one must possess. Empathy is a critical competence when building and managing a relationship. Building and handling relationship is largely an art but following best practices increases chances of succeeding

Finally, change management skills are a critical part of social skills. Another continuous aspect of social interactions is changing. In any group setting, one or several members might leave or behave differently than the known behavioral set and these calls for change management competencies to avert fallouts in the group.

Exercise

a. Use a past experience, explain how some of the social skills were exhibited or not exhibited.

Conclusion

In summary, the author managed to take the reader through want is emotional intelligence and how it differs with other related concepts such as social intelligence and emotional intelligence. The author provided an exercise at the end of each chapter to enable the reader to reflect. The exercises are easy to do and at most involve only two questions. Using easy and relatable examples, the author hopes to make the reader realize that emotional intelligence is manifesting in and around us. The approach of the author on the topic is from a neutral point of view and this lets the reader make a judgment on the suggested value of emotional intelligence.

Finally, this book weaves together what would be separate books on emotional intelligence making this book an interpreted approach to emotional intelligence. Throughout the book, the author maintains the simplicity of language and pays attention to the applicability of the suggested areas of emotional intelligence to the workplace, individually and social events. The content of the book has been carefully evaluated to ensure that is relevant and applicable in all contexts. Against this backdrop, this book can be seen as a manual and personal assessment of applicable emotional intelligent for individuals and groups.

If you found this book useful in anyway, a review is always appreciated.

www.ingramcontent.com/pod-product-compliance
Lightning Source LLC
Chambersburg PA
CBHW060400080526
44583CB00012B/402